MARCO POLO

BARCELONA

FRANCE
SWITZERLAND
ITALY
Bilbao
ANDORRA
Madrid
SPAIN
Barcelona
Corsica (F)
Valencia
Mallorca
The Balearics
Sardinia (I)
The Mediterranean
ALGERIA

The best Insider Tips → p. 4

INSIDER TIP

Best of... → p. 6

Sightseeing → p. 26

Food & drink → p. 58

SYMBOLS

INSIDER TIP	Insider Tip
★	Highlight
●●●●	Best of ...
☼	Scenic view
☺	Responsible travel: for ecological or fair trade aspects
(*)	Telephone numbers that are not toll-free

PRICE CATEGORIES HOTELS

Expensive	over 180 euros
Moderate	120–180 euros
Budget	under 120 euros

Prices for a double room without breakfast

PRICE CATEGORIES RESTAURANTS

Expensive	over 40 euros
Moderate	20–40 euros
Budget	under 20 euros

Prices for a main course with starter, but without drinks

On the cover: Parc Güell – Dream views from a fairytale park p. 53 | Beach life in the city p. 35

CONTENTS

Shopping → p. 70

Entertainment → p. 78

Where to stay → p. 86

Street atlas → p. 120

DID YOU KNOW?
Barça: much more than just a football club → p. 21
Keep fit! → p. 44
Relax & enjoy → p. 48
Books & films → p. 55
Gourmet restaurants → p. 62
Local specialities → p. 68
Luxury hotels → p. 90
Currency converter → p. 111

MAPS IN THE GUIDEBOOK
(122 A1) Page numbers and coordinates refer to the atlas and the map of Barcelona and surrounding area on p. 138/139
(0) Site/address located off the map.
Coordinates are also given for places that are not marked on the street atlas.
For a map of local transport options see the back cover.

INSIDE BACK COVER:
PULL-OUT MAP →

PULL-OUT MAP _ℳ_
(_ℳ A–B 2–3_) Refers to the removable pull-out map

The best MARCO POLO Insider Tips

Our top 15 Insider Tips

INSIDER TIP **Medieval skyscrapers**
Together, the *Plaça del Rei* and the fascinating silhouette of the historic royal palace form a splendid ensemble in the evening sun → **p. 33**

INSIDER TIP **Seeing stars with Michelin**
Spain's star chef Martín Berasategui will spoil you with exquisite cuisine at reasonable prices at his *Loidi* gourmet bistro → **p. 64**

INSIDER TIP **Angled columns**
Gaudí's unfinished masterpiece: the *Cripta de la Colonia Güell* is among the genius architect's most daring designs → **p. 56**

INSIDER TIP **Green maze**
Wander on winding paths between bridges and fountains, marble temples and small lakes in the *Parc del Laberint* → **p. 53**

INSIDER TIP **Feast like the monks**
Caelum will sell you heavenly delicacies from Spanish monasteries – in historic cellar vaults from a different world → **p. 73**

INSIDER TIP **Travel back in time**
For Gothic architecture and divine delectation head for the *Museu-Monestir Pedralbes* monastery with its magnificent cloister (photo above) → **p. 53**

INSIDER TIP **Catalan pick-me-up at the delicatessen**
Hearty sustenance with tapas, sausage and wine at the *La Pineda* deli → **p. 74**

INSIDER TIP **On wooden benches in the courtyard café**
Refreshment with a bohemian touch in the cosy *Bar de L'Antic Teatre* – an oasis only a few steps from the madding crowd → **p. 60**

BEST OF ...

FOR FREE

● *Art behind wavy walls*

Take a look behind the scenes in Antoni Gaudí's famous residential building, the *Casa Milà*. To get to the free changing exhibitions on the first floor, take the unique 'snail' staircase – saving the entrance fee → p. 37

● *Music by master-class students*

Whether you're into early music, classical or jazz: listening to the pupils and master-class students of the *Catalan conservatory* at their rehearsals in the auditorium is usually free → p. 53

● *Magical light and water show on Montjuïc*

At the weekend, Barcelona's famous Art Deco fountain *Font Màgica* at the foot of Montjuïc unfolds its charms: in a free evening spectacle, gigantic jets of water in all colours burst into the sky → p. 100

● *Picasso on a Sunday*

A number of museums open their doors for free on Sunday afternoons from 3pm; amongst them the *Museu Picasso*, the most visited museum in Barcelona. If you choose the first Sunday in the month for your visit, you'll even have all day to explore for free → p. 53

● *At home in trendy clubs*

Have your name put on the right guest list, and party in the hippest and most exclusive clubs in town – for free. Shaz's guest list even gives you free access to the trendy *Shoko* lounge club, right on the beach (photo left) → p. 84

● *Modernist and modern*

From outside and in, the *Caixa Forum* is a very special art experience that won't cost you a penny: the imposing Art Nouveau building, a spectacularly restored textile factory, houses one of Europe's most important collections of contemporary art → p. 50

● ● ● ● ● Dots in guidebook refer to 'Best of ...' tips

● *Gaudí's divine temple*
Sagrada Família (photo right) is the world-famous symbol of Barcelona. Let the gigantic columns and spectacular interior of the huge nave consecrated by the Pope work their magic on you → p. 40

● *Fairy-tale gardens above the city*
Enchanting park with panoramic views: when creating the *Parc Güell*, Antoni Gaudí let his imagination run riot and revealed his universal genius as architect, landscape designer – and a pioneer of recycling → p. 53

● *Mediterranean spirit*
Enjoy the flair of the Mediterranean metropolis on one of its many squares with a coffee or a cool beer. *Plaça de la Vila* and *Plaça de la Virreina* in Gràcia are particularly atmospheric → p. 47

● *Catalan-Caribbean sounds*
The *rumba catalana*, an explosive mix of flamenco, Caribbean rhythms and rock, is the music of the Catalan gitanos and super-trendy in Barcelona right now. Meet the best bands every Wednesday at the *Sala Apolo* club's 'Rumba night' → p. 23, 84

● *Popular mayhem*
Throw yourself into the crowd on the famous *Rambla* – tourists and theatre-goers, culture vultures and purveyors of kitsch souvenirs, dolled-up opera-goers and agile waiters → p. 43

● *Lavish Art Nouveau splendour*
Blossoms, tendrils, dragon heads: if you want to experience Catalan Art Nouveau in all its glory, head for the *Palau de la Música Catalana*, the most ornate monument to modernisme → p. 31

● *Towering humans*
At traditional *castells,* a popular sport in Catalonia, you are not only allowed to watch balance artists training – the courageous may even join in → p. 19, 105

ONLY IN

BEST OF ...

● **Innovative and interactive**
In the *CosmoCaixa* science museum, one of the largest and most exciting of its kind in Europe, you can cross a tropical rainforest, look at the stars or create a sandstorm → **p. 50**

● **Experience Art Nouveau living**
Make yourself comfortable in an authentic Art Nouveau flat: in *Casa Batlló* on the fine boulevard of Passeig de Gràcia an audioguide takes you through the building designed by Antoni Gaudí → **p. 37**

● **In the belly of Barcelona**
In the city's most beautiful market hall, the *Boqueria* (photo above), the enticing piles of fruit, vegetable and spices, the fresh fish and seafood help you forget bad weather. Take advantage of the location and eat right there at one of the stalls – amongst locals → **p. 74**

● **Amongst sharks**
This large *Aquàrium* allows you to cross below a gigantic oceanarium with sunfish and sharks, admire coral reefs and learn about flora and fauna of the world's oceans without getting wet → **p. 46**

● **Catalan culture – an overview**
The *Museum of Catalan Art* makes it easy to spend a dull day in style: this way you have time to admire the world-famous collection of Romanesque frescoes, pioneering paintings by Picasso and exciting contemporary art → **p. 52**

● **Fine food for a sweet tooth**
Here is the way to stay dry on the Rambla even in the rain: take to the enchanting Art Nouveau café *Pastelería Escribà* to enjoy the finest delicacies from Barcelona's longest-established patisserie → **p. 74**

RAIN

RELAX AND CHILL OUT
Take it easy and spoil yourself

● *Balm for body and soul*
Treat yourself to a short massage at *Masajes a 1000*; don't even worry about booking in advance, just turn up when you feel like it → **p. 48**

● *Chilling at the CDLC beach club*
Reclining on cool leather loungers under Bedouin tents, with a view of the Mediterranean in an Indian-inspired interior: at the *Carpe Diem Lounge Club* relaxing is an experience for all the senses → **p. 80**

● *Divine delectation*
In the historic cellar vault of the *Caelum* enjoy homemade delicacies from Spanish convents by candlelight to the sound of classical music or low-key jazz. The café was laid out following feng shui principles – an oasis of harmony and relaxation → **p. 73**

● *Shipshape?*
A harbour trip aboard a traditional wooden barge or a modern catamaran lets you breathe in a fresh breeze and observe the city from the water, where all is calm → **p. 110**

● *Fill up with some energy in the park*
Recuperate from treading the cobblestones in one of the city's most beautiful parks, the *Parc de la Ciutadella*. Take a little boat trip on the lake or observe the apes at the zoo → **p. 35**

● *Calming view of infinity*
Barcelona's mile-long sandy bathing beach (photo below) is a relaxation zone in itself: you can stroll along the palm-lined promenade, swim, sunbathe – and take a nightcap in one of the beach clubs or beach bars → **p. 48**

● *Float away from gravity*
Goodbye tensions, hello happiness: in the *Flotarium*, float in salt-saturated water inside a futuristic bathing capsule, extending all four limbs without a care in the world → **p. 48**

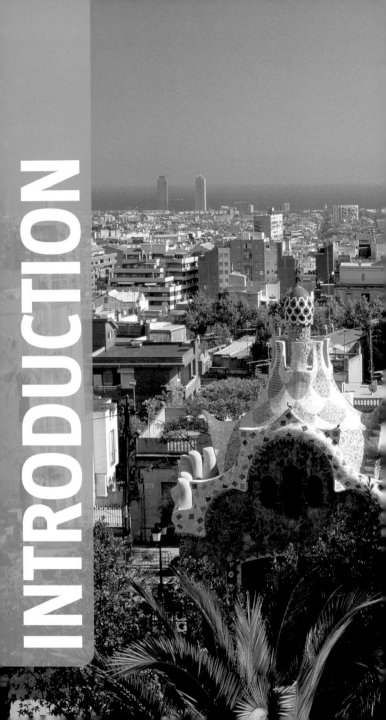

INTRODUCTION

DISCOVER BARCELONA!

Visitors arriving by plane can get their first overview of Barcelona when the plane is preparing for landing. Up front is the Mediterranean, on the sides the city is bounded by gentle mountain ranges. Striking high-rises and ultramodern towers stand out from the maze of alleyways that make up the Gothic core . Right next to it you can make out the chessboard-like street grid of the Art Nouveau quarter Eixample. There's no doubt about it: Barcelona (1.5 million inhabitants) is a place of fascinating contrasts. This major design metropolis with its award-winning post-modern buildings boasts the largest historic city centre in Europe after Naples, where you can lose yourself for hours.

Most flats however are compact to tiny – and exorbitantly expensive, as land between the mountains and the sea is becoming scarce while the city has turned into a Mediterranean trend metropolis – following the motto 'newer, bigger, prettier'. At the same time even zeitgeist-chasing trendsetters feel deeply connected to Catalan tradition and history. In any case, the Catalans know better than maybe any other

Photo: Parc Güell

nation how to integrate contradictions. Take the Catalan bourgeoisie, which built one of the most magnificent Art Nouveau quarters in the world. Lavishly ornamented buildings, sensual artistic universes – but behind the façades there was always a sober merchant spirit hard at work. This is not to say that the Catalans aren't creative. On the contrary, the city has never been short of innovative energy. It is constantly on the move and reinventing itself afresh. All it takes is some great event, in order to achieve something pioneering or a task that was long waiting to be tackled. It was like that for the World Exhibition of 1888, which awakened the city from its Sleeping Beauty slumber and heralded a new departure into an age of blossoming Art Nouveau. For this show the grounds around the Ciutadella Park were created. In 1929, parts of the city were again completely turned inside out to get ready for the second World Exhibition – this time it was the turn of Montjuïc.

Relaxing along miles of sandy beach

The Olympic Games of 1992 then gifted Barcelona a completely new city: the depressing heritage of 40 years of dictatorship were swept aside, and the Mediterranean metropolis, renewed all over, started its ascent to become a mecca for architects, urban planners and tourists. Barcelona has opened itself towards the sea: one of the most popular achievements is the miles-long sandy bathing beach. At the weekend in particular Barcelonetas stroll, jog, bike or skate along the palm-fringed promenade, treat themselves to a paella with sea view or relax with a drink in beach bars and clubs.

North of the Olympic village, the *Poble Nou* quarter is being turned from a gigantic industrial ruin into Barcelona's ultimate high-tech quarter: a new cultural and pub scene clusters around imposing company headquarters, innovation centres and production studios, partly in extensive factory lofts. The eye-catcher of this brave new architectural world is the huge phallic skyscraper of *Torre Agbar* – shimmering in all colours, this was a design by Jean Nouvel for Barcelona's water company.

So: when the image of the city is in question, no expenses are spared. This also holds true for the revitalisation of the northernmost district on the Mediterranean shore on the estuary of the Besó, around the extended main artery of the Diagonal. Over the past few years one of the most exclusive quarters in town has been arising here, the *Diagonal Mar*, with exclusive offices and residential accommodation, as well as tall design hotels. The most recent coup is the idiosyncratic seat of the Spanish telecommunications company, the *Edificio Telefónica Diagonal 00* by architect Enric Massip Bosch, which corkscrews into the Mediterranean sky like a diamond. Another eyecatcher is the huge bright-blue triangle opposite, the Forum *(Edifici Fòrum)*. This is one of Europe's largest congress and exhibition centres, designed by Swiss star architects Herzog & de Meuron.

> **Catalan was banned under Franco**

The Catalan propensity to the grand gesture has its roots in history. In the 19th century, nothing was too ostentatious for the bourgeoisie, whether materially or intellectually wealthy: especially anything that put one over the unloved central power in Madrid. At that time already, the economic powerhouse of Catalonia wanted to overtake politically dominant Castile – at least in art and architecture. This might go some way towards explaining the love of lavish ornamentation displayed by *modernisme*, the Catalan version of Art Nouveau. Everything was supposed to be even bigger, even more splendid and beautiful than in the Spanish capital. Not much has changed since then; only that instead of modernist dragon heads we now have hypermodern design. The thorn of history is still deeply embedded in Catalan skin: since the 16th century, Catalonia, once a medieval global power, has time

With its yachts and fancy restaurants the old port area projects a high-class image

and again had to accept central Spanish supremacy. This happened most recently under the dictatorship of General Franco: the *generalísimo* wanted to tidy up the rebellious bastion in the north – and annihilate any sign of its identity, starting with the Catalan language, which was banned. The Franco dictatorship may have ended in 1975, but its consequences still affect the Catalans. Meanwhile, some 75 per cent of the population speak Catalan, though a good half of the locals prefer Spanish in day-to-day life. Even so: perfect *català* has become the most important skill required for employment.

Mediterranean laid-back lifestyle

Distrust and prejudices of the Catalans towards Madrid – and vice versa of course – can only be overcome gradually. Anyone who has witnessed the impromptu mass congregation and frenetic celebrations on the Rambla after a victory of FC Barcelona over archrival Real Madrid knows that this is about more than just football. In Catalonia there is still a sense of being the victim of centralising injustice. Not without reason – however, over time, the role of eternal victim has become maybe a bit too comfortable. Whether financial worries or bad planning: it's always Madrid's fault.

Add to this the Catalan character: on the one hand marked by a laid-back Mediterranean lifestyle, on the other looking towards Europe. The Catalans have always felt closer to their northern neighbours than to the Iberian Peninsula. As the northernmost metropolis of the south, Barcelona is often called the north's southernmost city – and that's true. Which doesn't mean that some contrasts always just disappear. Sometimes, they even clash quite dramatically, in the Old Town for instance, more and more of which has been entirely redeveloped in recent years. In the completely renovated Old Town quarter of Raval traces of the demi-monde of whores, fraudsters and gangsters that inspired the French writer Jean Genet to write 'A Thief's Journal' are still visible in the legendary *Barri Xino*, the port and red-light district of Barcelona. A few paces on, the hip cultural and bar scene around the Museum of Contemporary Art and the fancy new boulevard of Rambla del Raval have changed the picture entirely.

This is not only for the good: overdue modernisation also brought property sharks, speculation, luxury hotels and the chic set into this traditional residential quarter. To the increasing annoyance of the population, which complains that Barcelona is being developed more and more to suit the needs of wealthy trendsetters and tourists. While their quarters lack important infrastructure, they see ever more luxury hotels rising on their doorsteps – for example the 26-storey W Hotel in the shape of a gigantic sail right on Barceloneta beach.

Now the inhabitants are getting organised in citizens' movements 'to save the Old Town'. In Barceloneta they want to stop their legendary fishing village, where neighbours still greet each other by name in the streets, from being turned into the 'Miami of Europe'. They don't want the quarters of Santa Caterina and Sant Pere, where a hip arts and bar scene is growing up, to look like the trendy neighbouring quarter of El Born one day. There you'll find a lot of crafts and design, plenty of trendy eateries, and everything is nicely restored. However, residents can no longer find a drugstore or butcher for their shopping, and rents have become far too high for locals. Sant

Strolling along Barcelona's famous boulevard, the Rambla

Pere still has narrow alleys with the cast-iron lanterns that look like electric lighting hasn't been invented yet. And it would be truly sad if in the course of the necessary renovation, the rough charm of medieval walls were to disappear from the quarter – taking many of its inhabitants with them.

However, we're not there yet. Barcelona might cherish its stylish image, but that doesn't make the Catalan capital into a uniformly glossy modern city. Many corners of the city still have shops and bars that have survived

Highly styled design metropolis

the design fever. And there are still enough young creative people with plenty of subversive imagination to go against the grain of the emblematic *disseny barceloní*.

So: experience a place of exciting contrasts, always on the move – and always with a surprise up its sleeve. Don't be sad if you didn't manage to take it all in. Just tell yourself: 'next time'. Because those who leave Barcelona usually have a firm idea that they'll be back.

WHAT'S HOT

1 Dining in style

Involve all the senses Enjoy hearty fare, a loungey atmosphere and a view of the city *(Mirador del Migdia)* at *La Caseta del Migdia* on Montjuïc. Another high point above Barcelona is the *Torre d'Alta Mar*. Situated nearly 250 ft above sea level *(Passeig Joan de Borgò, 88)* and boasting luxurious wallpapers, chandeliers and furniture, the international restaurant *Rococó* truly lives up to its name *(Av. Francesc Cambó, 30–36)*.

Skaters' heaven

One board, four wheels Barcelona boasts the title of 'skate capital of the world'. Highlight of the year is the *Contest Barcelona Extreme (www.movistarbarcelonaextreme.com)*, but throughout the year professional skaters congregate for international meets. UK legend Tom Penny is based here too. To watch the youngsters hone their moves, head for the Museum of Contemporary Art on Tuesday and Friday, or on any day for the skatepark, stairs and ledges between the Forum Metro stop and the ocean.

2

Eco mobile

3

Sustainable transport 2011 saw the first edition of the *ECO sèries* of the *Catalan Motor Racing Federation* where ecological vehicles are presented to a large audience. The race is intended to effect an image change *(www.ecoraces.net, photo)*. The ecological and comfortable way to get around is a Segway tour *(www.segwaytours.cat)* or an e-bike *(Barcelona Electric Bicycle, Ausiàs Marc, 155, www.beb.com.es)*. Travelling by plane, your arrival at least is eco-friendly: Terminal 1 of the *El Prat* airport runs on solar power. Guided tours through the sustainable airport can be arranged *(tel. 9 32 59 62 02, Prat de Llobregat, www.aena.es)*.

Upcycling

Hello goodbye   At *Vaho's*, old tarps or plastic canisters are made into cool bags or cushions *(Plaça de Sant Josep Oriol, 3, www.vaho.ws, photo)*. Trendsetters purchase bags for laptops, cosmetics or school gear at *Demano's* where every piece made of discarded advertising banners or foils is a one-off *(Carrer dels Carders, 14, www.demano.net)*. Drap-Art too is a past master of recycling. This non-profit organisation runs a workshop where new things are created from all kinds of reject materials. Kitchen implements, bits of fabric and wire for example are turned into marionettes and other works of art. Exhibitions of such items take place on a regular basis *(Groc, 1, www.drapart.org)*.

Towards the future

Architecture   The days of the old industries have now passed. In Poble Nou, the project *22@Barcelona (www.22barcelona.com)* is creating a pioneering quarter. Good ideas and the requisite funds are in place to create quality spaces for living and working. Obsolete industrial buildings have been integrated into the project, such as the new audiovisual media centre *(www.parcbarcelonamedia.com)*. Completely new is the Barcelona-Sagrera railway station, which is being built to designs by star architect Frank Gehry *(www.barcelona sagrera.com)*. However, even the high-tech quarter doesn't want to totally deny its past. The legendary *Razzmatazz* club is also at home here and enjoying a second wind of popularity *(Pamplona, 88)*.

IN A NUTSHELL

BULLFIGHTING

To the Spanish, bullfighting is sacred – the Catalans find it rather suspect, however, more and more of them rejecting this centuries-old tradition as cruelty to animals. In 2010 a historic decision was taken in the regional parliament: Catalonia became the first region on the Spanish mainland to ban bullfighting from 2012. True, few *corridas* were taking place in Barcelona – younger people especially have little time for the bloody spectacle. However, it is expected that the ban will have repercussions on other regions. Catalonia will however keep the regional tradition of the *correbous*, where the bull is chased through the streets wearing a torch on his horns – and no bloody ending.

CASTELLS

Popular sports and expression of Catalan national pride: *castells,* towers made up of human bodies, are a firm part of any celebration. The *castellers* build their daring figures up to ten levels high (nearly 50 ft) – following exact mathematical calculations. The strongest occupy the lower ranks, the younger and lighter scramblers form the upper storeys, and at the end a child climbs the 'summit'. A perfect pyramid finishes with a seamless come-down, which is also judged when the associations, *colles de castellers,* try to trump each other at competitions, to the sound of drum rolls and traditional Catalan music.

In Barcelona *castellers* usually perform on the city hall square, Plaça de Sant Jaume.

Photo: Casa Milà/La Pedrera

Culture yesterday and today: the people of Barcelona are music-lovers with a keen eye for beauty

The first figures emerged in the late 17th century, when people climbed on each others' shoulders at the end of popular dances. From the 18th century the dancers tried to surpass each other through ever more daring formations, and the dance element soon fell by the wayside. The *castellers* experienced their heyday in the 19th century. As a symbol of Catalan national culture they were banned during the military dictatorship under General Franco. Today, the custom is again a staple of popular fairs and celebrations

– and was even placed under UNESCO World Heritage protection in 2011. ● At the *Castellers de Barcelona* association *(www.castellersdebarcelona.cat)* you can not only watch the training, but also take part if you dare – for free.

CATALAN

Officially, Catalonia is bilingual: all notices, forms, signposts, etc. are supposed to be written both in Spanish and in Catalan. In theory. In practice, the Catalans prefer their own language to

Spanish, which can sometimes cause confusion. If you react to a question or a greeting in Spanish, Catalan-speakers will usually automatically switch to Spanish.

Bizarre roof landscape on Gaudí's Casa Milà

Catalan is spoken by around 6 million people: along the Mediterranean coast between Perpignan and Alicante, on the Balearics, in Andorra – and in the Sardinian town of Alghero.

DESIGN

Barcelona's reputation as a hotbed of international design (with stars such as Mariscal or Oscar Tusquets) is undisputed now. We've got past the boom of the 1980s and early 1990s, when design was the be-all and end-all, whether in cultural or dress issues, restaurants or clubs. Design rapidly became a symbol for the image and identity of the brave new – and finally modern – post-Franco world. Today, the aesthetic renewal trip has calmed down. The consequences are still tangible though: like when you end up sitting on one of those award-winning but desperately uncomfortable bar stools that have names like 'Frenesí' (madness). Thankfully, the idea that an object should not only be beautiful but also useful, comfortable and eco-friendly is increasingly gaining ground.

ECOLOGY

The green eco wave has made it across the Pyrenees and rolled into Barcelona with a delay of some ten years. Now, the city wants to create a green image for itself. Indeed, first successes can be reported. More and more city buses now get around using biofuel. In terms of solar legislation, Barcelona is actually a European leader: large new construction projects – whether residential buildings, offices or hotels – have to meet part of their energy needs through solar cells or photovoltaic installations. The recycling idea is also slowly gaining ground: rubbish is increasingly thrown into separate containers. And while up to a few years ago, it was not well seen amongst Catalans to be buying anything 'pre-loved', now ever more second-hand shops are opening. Even in Barcelona, using the label ecológico or *fair trade* brings in clients to shops or restaurants. The first chain stores are offering their own organic products, and organic supermarkets, whilst still relatively expensive, are becoming more popular.

ANTONI GAUDÍ

A genius or a madman, that was one teacher's assessment of Gaudí as a young student of architecture. Visitors to buildings by this master architect and craftsman, born the son of a coppersmith in 1852 in Reus near Tarragona, might come to the conclusion that both are true. Gaudí did in fact rapidly move away from the paths of the architecture of his time as it was taught at university. The profuse organic forms of his buildings, their fantastic colours, force of form and the exuberant imagination of his utopian designs upset many of his contemporaries. It's hardly surprising that all his life he was short of official commissions and awards. Instead, it was private patrons of the arts such as Eusebio Güell who recognised Gaudí's genius and supported his work – today, Parc Güell, Palau Güell and Casa Milà form part of the Unesco World Heritage list.

Gaudí's life was full of contradictions. As a young man, he had a reputation as a dandy who enjoyed life to the full and was enthusiastic about revolutionary ideas and moved in atheist circles. Despite this, he started building the Sagrada Família church, which is still unfinished, at the age of 30. In old age he dedicated his entire creative energy to the church, living an increasingly ascetic life. In 1926, the 'Dante of architecture' was killed by a tram.

MODERNISME

Modernisme, the Catalan variant of Art Nouveau which entered the scene in the late 19th century, was not only the expression of a rebellion against the geometry and straight lines of industrial society. Most of all it offered a suitable aesthetic framework for the spirit of the upwardly mobile bourgeoisie. In decoratively exuberant designs the Catalan bourgeoisie – wealthy but politically dominated by Madrid – found an effec-

BARÇA: MUCH MORE THAN JUST A FOOTBALL CLUB

When FC Barcelona plays archrival Real Madrid, it's the mental state of the Catalans that's at stake: after a victory the entire city enters a state of euphoria, but slides into a collective depression after a defeat. *Barça*, you see, has always been more than a football club: a popular symbol of Catalan confidence, especially against the unloved central power vested in Madrid.

Founded in 1890, Barça is one of the world's oldest football clubs and boasts one of the largest fan bases in the world, as well as the largest football museum housed in the world's second-largest stadium, Camp Nou. When Barça is pitted against Real Madrid, you've hardly a hope in hell of getting tickets, but with less spectacular games you might be lucky. Online advance sales start a month before the match, phone sales 14 days before. *Museum and stadium Nov–March Mon–Sat 10am–6.30pm, Sun 10am–1.30pm, April–Oct Mon–Sat 10am–7pm, Sun 10am–1pm | admission museum 8.50 euros, museum and stadium together 19 euros | Camp Nou, entrance 9 | Aristides Maillol* **(126 B3) (** *D 6) | tel. 9 34 96 36 00 | www.fcbarcelona.com | Metro: Collblanc (L5)*

The Picasso Museum predominantly shows early works from his time in Barcelona

tive means of occupying the public stage and their own national style to mirror Catalans' reawakening confidence. The movement was not restricted to architecture, encompassing all areas of design, whether furniture, ceramics, jewellery or cast-iron. Its main protagonists were Josep Puig i Cadafalch, Lluís Domènech i Montaner and Antoni Gaudí. To gain an overview, why not follow the *Ruta del Modernisme (www.rutadelmodernisme. com)* put together by the tourist board, leading to over 100 important sights of Catalan Art Nouveau.

PABLO PICASSO

Whilst Picasso was born (in 1881) in Málaga in southern Spain, he is also considered a son of the city of Barcelona. The boy moved to the city in 1895 with his family, when his father got a job as teacher at La Llotja art academy. Even then, the artistic talents of the young Picasso were so obvious that he was accepted at the academy aged only 13. It is said that he completed the work neces-

sary for acceptance, scheduled to take a month, in one day. In any case, he was immediately allowed to leapfrog a few classes.

The family's flat was only a few paces from the Academy in the direction of the port, above the arcades of the *Porxos d'en Xifre* building. From the terrace, Picasso observed and painted the sea, the Mediterranean light, the roofs and the alleyways of the Old Town. Many of these early works are today on view at the city's Picasso Museum. At 14, the young painter moved into his first own studio. Soon he belonged to the vibrant artists' and bohemian scene of Barcelona, which felt closer to avant-garde Paris than conservative, sedate Madrid. The meeting place was the *Els Quatre Gats* restaurant, which, following the model of *Le Chat Noir* in Paris, was opened in a building designed by Art Nouveau architect Puig i Cadafalch and is still in existence today. This is where Picasso had his first exhibition, in 1900 – and for which he designed the vignettes on the menu.

In the red-light district of the Old Town, around Carrer Avinyó, the young man collected pertinent experiences, inspiring his famous painting Les Demoiselles d'Avignon. Although Picasso moved to the French capital for good in 1904, his ten year-period in Barcelona remained a lasting influence on his work.

RUMBA CATALANA

A mix of flamenco, Afro-Caribbean music and rock 'n' roll: the ● *rumba catalana* emerged in the 1950s in the quarters of Gràcia, Hostafrancs and Sant Antoni, home to the Catalan *gitanos*, who have lived here for over 200 years. With the rumba they invented their own musical style – and a new way of playing the guitar using not only the strings but also beating the wooden body of the instrument. With the summer hit 'Borriquito', the Catalan rumba star Peret even jumped to the top of the 1971 international charts. For the past few years a new generation of musicians has been modernising the *rumba catalana*, in a search

of their own identity as *gitanos* and Catalans. The new sound from Barcelona is totally hip, not only in the city itself.

SENY AND RAUXA

In the same way that Barcelona is characterised by charming contrasts, the character and spirit of its inhabitants are marked by two completely opposite characteristics. One the one hand, the Catalans have common sense, a sense of community and business sense, allied to ambition and discipline. On the other hand, all this reason can suddenly tip over into a state of intoxicated excitement: *seny* and *rauxa* (pronounced: rowsha) are the names of these two extremes. They produced the economic prosperity of the region as well as artistic geniuses such as Salvador Dalí and Joan Miró, political pragmatism as well as major anarchist uprisings. To this day the Catalans harbour an ancient yearning for Europe, 'the north' – and a deeply Mediterranean mentality at the same time.

TRAFFIC

Often, the sky over Barcelona is bright blue. But this Mediterranean idyll is misleading. There are many days when air pollution levels are way above EU limits. Every day, millions of private vehicles struggle through Barcelona and the suburbs, despite a good public transport system. Low-emission zones or driving bans such as in other large European cities exist only on paper. The 80 km/h speed limit on city motorways had hardly been introduced when it had to be abolished again because the population was protesting. The car is sacred to the Catalans. At least they now occasionally climb into the saddle of a bike: automatic *Bicing* stations with rental bikes are everywhere in Barcelona now.

THE PERFECT DAY

Barcelona in 24 hours

10:00am RAMBLA INTO RAVAL

To start off, take Barcelona's famous boulevard, the *Rambla* → p. 43, at a stroll from Plaça de Catalunya towards the port. Make a quick detour to the right into the hip quarter of *Raval* → p. 41, past the Museum of Contemporary Art and across the patio of the Centre of Contemporary Culture. In the romantic courtyard of the Gothic complex of *Antic Hospital de la Santa Creu* → p. 42 it's easy to forget the tourists.

11:00am MEDITERRANEAN MARKET HALL

Time to hit the scrum again. At the *Boqueria market* → p. 74, the 'belly of Barcelona', have a taste of the Mediterranean spirit. The famous market hall is a mecca for gourmets, and the enchanting Art Nouveau patisserie *Pastelería Escribá* → p. 74 (photo left) the ideal place for the first coffee break.

12:00pm PICTURESQUE SQUARES AND ALLEYWAYS

After a look at the opera house Gran Teatre del Liceu, head into the *Gothic Quarter (Barri Gòtic)* → p. 28 (photo below) via the picturesque 'twin squares' of *Plaça de Sant Josep Oriol and Plaça del Pi* → p. 32. Past the church of Santa María del Pi and via the Carrer dels Banys Nous, approach the alleys of the Jewish quarter of El Call – after a quick peek of the idyllic Old Town square of *Plaça de Sant Felip Neri* → p. 32.

01:00pm GOTHIC AND ROMAN

You can't miss the Gothic *Cathedral* → p. 29. Step into this imposing church to admire the beautiful choir stalls and the enchanting cloister. Via *Plaça del Rei* → p. 33 with the royal palace and the medieval guard tower carry on to the *Museu d'Història de la Ciutat* → p. 30. Even if you don't have time for a visit, take a look through the windows to make out the Roman ruins in underground Barcelona.

02:00pm LUNCH ON THE MARKET

You've really earned your lunch now: browsing the stalls of the historic market hall of *Mercat de Santa Caterina* → p. 49

provides you with fresh Mediterranean fare from simple tapas to a full meal. Thus fortified, the afternoon entertainment beckons.

03:00pm FAIRY-TALE PARK AND MEGA-TEMPLE

First take the Metro to *Parc Güell* → p. 53 (photo right). Antoni Gaudí's fantastic park provides you with a fabulous panoramic view across the city. Once more into the Metro, and you're at Gaudí's world-famous church, *Sagrada Família* → p. 40. A must! The eastern façade, completed by Gaudí, and the spectacular interior of the gigantic nave with its massive columns are particularly worth seeing.

06:00pm ART NOUVEAU MILE

Lovers of Catalan Art Nouveau will not want to miss the Passeig de Gràcia: Barcelona's fine and fancy boulevard is lined with some of the most important Art Nouveau buildings: Antoni Gaudí's *Casa Milà/La Pedrera* and *Casa Batlló,* the *Casa Amatller* by Josep Puig i Cadafalch and Domènech i Montaner's *Casa Lleó Morera* → p. 36 – 38. After so much ornamentation your stomach might want something substantial: it's only a few minutes on foot to the delicious snacks served at *Tapas,24* → p. 61.

08:00pm MARITIME EVENING

Relax with a stroll or aperitif on the *beach* → p. 48. Afterwards, enjoy a meal at one of the typical eateries of the Barceloneta fishing village, such as *La Bombeta* → p. 69. You might be lucky and get tickets for a concert at the *Palau de la Música Catalana* → p. 31, p. 85 with its incomparable Art Nouveau splendour.

10:00pm LAST DRINK

Conclude the day with a drink with panoramic views from the *roof terrace of a fancy hotel* → p. 79 or in the legendary cocktail bar *Boadas* → p. 79 on the Rambla.

Metro to the starting point: L1, L3
Stop: Plaça de Catalunya
Taking the Metro is inexpensive in Barcelona: a single journey costs 1.45 euros

SIGHTSEEING

CITY WHERE TO START?
Plaça de Catalunya (123 D2)
(*[map] J 9*): from here stroll down Barcelona's famous boulevard of La Rambla. To the right of the promenade lies the Raval quarter, on the other side the Gothic Quarter with its many sights. The Modernist monuments on Passeig de Gràcia too are only a few minutes' walk away. Below Plaça de Catalunya there are well-signposted multi-storey car parks. The Metro lines L1 and L3 stop here, as well as the FGC suburban train and a number of buses.

It was Miguel de Cervantes, no less, who had his Don Quijote character talk about Barcelona as possessed of a 'unique beauty'. Contemporary travellers won't fail to agree with the hapless knight's eulogy.

Where else do you find so many and various sights all in one place? The largest Gothic quarter after the one in Prague, the splendid monuments of *modernisme,* ultramodern creations by international star architects and designers, from Jean Nouvel to Norman Foster: Barcelona's image has been and still is determined through art and culture. And it is not only significant buildings that enchant visitors: art forms a natural part of city life, whether in the streets or on squares,

Photo: Plaça Reial

The Middle Ages, modernisme and Postmodernism: take your time to discover the beauty of this Mediterranean metropolis

in houses, courtyards, parks or patios. An eminently enthusiastic American art historian once crowned it 'Europe's largest open-air museum'.

If you want to get close to the much-vaunted beauty of Barcelona, try and make time to discover the countless decorative details of the city. Not forgetting of course Barcelona's over 50 museums and collections, ranging from world-famous Romanesque frescoes to the football trophies of FC Barcelona.

Be aware though that on Mondays and Sunday afternoons many museums are closed! In July and August some will open in the evening hours when it is less hot, sometimes offering special guided tours, with a refreshing drink even. For more information visit the Palau de la Virreina *(Rambla, 99 | tel. 9 33 01 77 75 | www.bcn.es/icub)* or check with the information points of the tourist board *(www.barcelonaturisme.com)*.

The map shows the location of the most interesting districts. There is a detailed map of each district on which each of the sights described is numbered.

BARRI GÒTIC

With its architectural splendour, the ★ *Barri Gòtic*, the 'heart of Barcelona', is a testimony to Catalonia's heyday as a Mediterranean power.

Most buildings and monuments date back to the 14th and 15th centuries, when the citizens' wealth led to a construction boom. Only once Barcelona lost its primacy to Castile in the 16th century did the Gothic Quarter start to decline. The historic buildings were given an exemplary restoration as part of the Olympic urban redevelopment. However, to this day many residential buildings are run-down. On the other hand, for a long time now this old part of town too has

attracted the attentions of urban renovation officers and architects, who in their wake brought the usual speculators and property sharks who are pushing the resident population out of their cheap accommodation: old people, students, artists or immigrants. Alongside curious corner shops, smoky bars or barbers' shops, hip boutiques, chic cafés and trendy bars are opening up now. Still, you can gain a lively impression of the Catalans' history and attitude to life in the maze of the old quarter's alleyways and back lanes.

◼◻ CASA DE L'ARDIACA
(123 D4) (*ØJ 10*)

On the southern side of the Plaça de la Seu, the square in front of the cathedral, lies the Casa de l'Ardiaca, the house of the archdeacon. The 12th-century building restored in the 15th century is today the seat of the municipal archives. Take a look at the idyllic inner courtyard with its Gothic fountain. The pretty marble post box at the entrance *(Carrer del Bisbe)* was designed by Art Nouveau architect Lluís Domènech i Montaner.

2 CATEDRAL (CATHEDRAL) ★
(123 D4) (*J 10*)

Construction of this imposing church was started in the 11th century on the foundations of an Early Christian basilica destroyed by the Moors. However, it was only between 1298 and 1448 that the magnificent nave was given its current form, while the neo-Gothic main façade was only completed in 1890. The choir stalls in the centre of the church – a peculiarity of Spanish churches which were not only conceived for liturgical purposes – are exquisitely beautiful. One of the 29 side chapels mainly dating from the 16th and 17th centuries holds a crucifix that allegedly performs miracles. It is said to have helped gain victory against the Turks in the great sea battle of Lepanto. The cathedral served to spread not only God's fame, but also secular glory. It is dedicated to the martyr Santa Eulàlia, patron saint of the city, who was tortured to death in late Roman times. The saint is buried in an alabaster sarcophagus in the crypt below the high altar.

Also worth seeing is the enchanting cloister with small chapels, garden, a Gothic fountain and a flock of geese. The cloister gives access to the small *museum (daily 10am–12 noon and 5–7.30pm | admission 2 euros)* of the cathedral, which shows archaeological finds and Gothic altarpieces alongside liturgical objects. *Mon–Sat 8.30am–12.30pm and Mon–Fri 5.15–7pm | free admission | Visita Turística (no guided tour!) | Mon–Sat 1–4.45pm, Sun 2–4.45pm | 5 euros (incl. visit to the choir stalls, museum and elevator up the church tower) | Plaça de la Seu | www.cat edralbcn.org | Metro: Jaume I (L4)*

MARCO POLO HIGHLIGHTS

★ **Barri Gòtic**
The Gothic Quarter, a unique gem of medieval architecture → p. 28

★ **Catedral**
The zenith of Catalan Gothic → p. 29

★ **Palau de la Música Catalana**
Magnificent concert hall in Art Nouveau style: a feast for the eyes, not only for lovers of music → p. 31

★ **Museu Picasso**
A master painter's beginnings → p. 34

★ **Casa Milà/La Pedrera**
Gaudí's unforgettable architectural offering → p. 37

★ **Sagrada Família**
Masterpiece and eternal construction site → p. 40

★ **Rambla**
Boulevard and stage for Barcelona life → p. 43

★ **Fundació Joan Miró**
Miró's works in a Mediterranean ambience → p. 51

★ **Teatre-Museu Dalí**
Impressive detour to Figueres: works of art by the Surrealist painter in a theatre renovated by the master himself → p. 57

★ **Parc Güell**
Bizarre balcony and picturesque park above the city → p. 53

The work of many generations: construction of the Gothic cathedral took centuries

▮3▮ MUSEU D'HISTÒRIA DE LA CIUTAT (MUSEUM OF CITY HISTORY)
(123 D4) *(Ⓜ J 10)*

The museum telling the story of the city is housed in a Gothic palace, which was taken down at its original site piece by piece in 1931 and rebuilt on the Plaça del Rei. Excavations revealed remains of Barcelona's Roman past, founded by Augustus in 15 BC and called Barcino at that time: canalisation, streets, baths, worships and mosaic floors may be viewed in the cellar vaults of the museum on some 4000 m² of exhibition space, one of Europe's largest archaeological excavations. The upper floors show remains of the Roman city wall as well as exhibits from medieval and modern times. *April–Sept Tue–Sat 10am–8pm, Sun 10am–8pm, Oct–March Tue–Sat 10am–2pm and 4–7pm, Sun 10am–8pm | admission 7 euros incl. entry to Museu-Monestir Pedralbes, Sun from 3pm free admission |* *Plaça del Rei | www.museuhistoria.bcn. es | Metro: Jaume I (L4)*

▮4▮ MUSEU FREDERIC MARÈS
(123 D4) *(Ⓜ J 10)*

Sculptor Frederic Marès (1893–1991) was a passionate traveller and collector of art. This medieval building on the Plaça del Rei is where you can admire the collection he assembled. The sculpture section with works from Roman times and the Romanesque, Gothic, Renaissance and Baroque periods is one of Spain's most comprehensive collections. The uppermost floors house INSIDER TIP▶ the *Sentimental Museum*, a collection of odds and ends of daily life from the 15th century up to the present day. *Tue–Sat 10am–7pm, Sun 11am–8pm | admission 4.20 euros, every first Sun of the month and every Sun from 3pm free admission | Plaça Sant Iu, 5 | www.museumares.bcn. es | Metro: Jaume I (L4)*

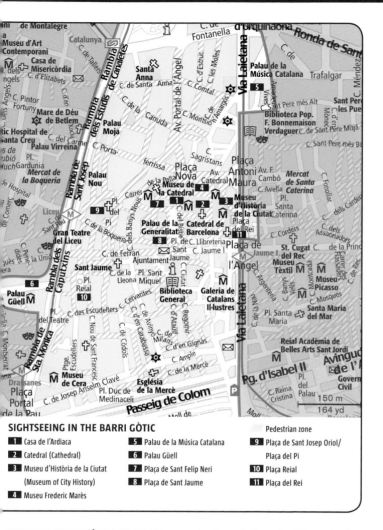

SIGHTSEEING IN THE BARRI GÒTIC

1 Casa de l'Ardiaca

2 Catedral (Cathedral)

3 Museu d'Història de la Ciutat
(Museum of City History)

4 Museu Frederic Marès

5 Palau de la Música Catalana

6 Palau Güell

7 Plaça de Sant Felip Neri

8 Plaça de Sant Jaume

Pedestrian zone

9 Plaça de Sant Josep Oriol/
Plaça del Pi

10 Plaça Reial

11 Plaça del Rei

5 PALAU DE LA MÚSICA CATALANA
★ ● (123 E3) (ℳ J 9)

Built by Lluís Domènech i Montaner between 1905 and 1908, this Palace of Music boasts the most unrestrained Art Nouveau style and forms a unique gem of *modernisme,* conceived as an 'Ode to Catalonia'. Opulently adorned street fa-

çades, towards Carrer Sant Pere més alt with mosaic-covered columns crowned by the busts of Bach, Beethoven, Wagner and Palestrina. The concave dome of colourful glass in the centre of the auditorium is of extraordinary beauty. The ceilings, walls and pillars of the space are covered in ornaments of flowers and tendrils in seemingly endless variations, as well as dragons' heads and other symbolic sculptures. No reservations taken, make sure you get your tickets in good time! *Guided tours daily 10.30am–3.30pm every 30 min, in July on many days to 7pm | admission 12 euros | Sant Pere més alt | tel. 932 95 72 00 | www.palaumusica.org | Metro: Urquinaona (L1, L4)*

6 PALAU GÜELL (122 B–C5) *(₥ H 10)*
An early work by Antoni Gaudí, which founded his reputation as one of the greatest architects and craftsmen of his time, the palace was built in 1889 for the patron and industrialist Eusebi Güell. The asymmetrical façade and the bizarre chimneys of the roof landscape already presage Gaudí's break with the geometrical forms that still dominated architecture at the time. *April–Sept Tue–Sun 10am–8pm, Oct–March 10am–5.30pm | admission 10 euros incl. audio guide, on first Sun of the month free of charge | Nou de la Rambla, 3 | www.palauguell.cat | Metro: Liceu (L3)*

7 INSIDERTIP ▶ PLAÇA DE SANT FELIP NERI (123 D4) *(₥ J 10)*
This picturesque little square in the Gothic Quarter forms an idyllic oasis of calm amidst the maze of the quarter's alleyways. Antoni Gaudí used to come here on his daily evening walks while building Sagrada Família. Worth seeing on the romantic square are the Baroque church of *Sant Felip Neri* and the Renaissance façade of the shoe museum *Museu del Calçat (Tue–Sun 11am–2pm | admission 2.50 euros). Metro: Catalunya (L1, L3)*

8 PLAÇA DE SANT JAUME (123 D4) *(₥ J 10)*
This square in the Gothic Quarter is where Catalan history was made and is still being made today. As far back as 2000 years ago, when Barcelona was still the Roman settlement of Barcino, this was the hub of municipal life. It was on this square that in 1931 the Catalan republic was proclaimed; from here the president of Catalunya, Josep Tarradellas, returning from exile in 1977, shouted out to the rapturous crowd his legendary sentence: *'Ja sóc aquí',* 'I'm back'. To this day, the Catalans congregate on Plaça de Sant Jaume to demonstrate, party or celebrate a victory of their FC Barcelona. Architecturally too, the square is remarkable. On one side stands the *Palau de la Generalitat,* seat of the autonomous Catalan regional government. The palace was erected between 1403 and 1630 around a Gothic core. Don't miss the pretty Sant Jordi (St George's) Chapel, the domed Sant Jordi Hall with ceiling paintings and the ornate Golden Hall, reached via the charming Courtyard of Orange Trees *(guided tours every second and fourth Sun 9am–1.30pm | free).* Opposite lies the *city hall (guided tours Sun 10.30am–1.30pm free).* The well-preserved Gothic part of the 14th-century Ajuntament with the splendid assembly hall of the *Consell de Cent* (Council of the Hundred) and its magnificent inner courtyard is worth seeing. The city hall's neoclassical façade dates from the 19th century. *Metro: Jaume I (L4)*

9 PLAÇA DE SANT JOSEP ORIOL/ PLAÇA DEL PI (122 C4) *(₥ H 10)*
The two squares around the Santa María del Pi church are amongst the most atmospheric in the city centre. The small bars and cafés with outdoor seating are great places to linger and watch life go by, followed by a nice little browse around the old shops. Every Sunday morning an arts market takes place here. *Metro: Liceu (L3)*

10 PLAÇA REIAL (122 C4–5) (*Ш H 10*)

One of the most beautiful squares of the city, the Royal Square was laid out between 1848 und 1859 on French models from the Napoleonic era. The arcaded complex of neo-Classical buildings was erected on top of a former Capuchin monastery. Its centre is occupied by the Three Graces fountain, which was later joined by modernist lanterns designed by Antoni Gaudí. After the square came down in the world and became a shelter for the drug trade and prostitution, it was renovated entirely in the early 1980s, and today has terrace cafés, restaurants, a jazz club, and discos. Watch out for pickpockets! *Metro: Liceu (L3)*

11 PLAÇA DEL REI (123 D4) (*Ш J 9*)

A unique architectural ensemble! The *Palau Reial Mayor,* the royal palace with its large *Saló del Tinell* banquet hall and imposing watchtower, the *Mirador del Rei Martí* (a kind of medieval high-rise), as well as the adjoining *Palau del Lloctinent* (Palace of the Lieutenant, Gothic façade, Renaissance inner courtyard) and the small Gothic chapel of *Santa Agata* (14th century) form a INSIDER TIP splendid backdrop, especially in the evening sunshine. The acoustics are also splendid – in the summer, interesting concerts take place here. The *Saló del Tinell*, the banquet hall of the royal palace, was where the Spanish kings received Columbus after his return from America. This was also where the Inquisition held court in the 15th century – those condemned as heretics were burned right on the square below. The interior of the palace is reached by the City History Museum at the other end of the Plaça del Rei.

LA RIBERA & PARC DE LA CIUTADELLA

The Ribera quarter was populated in medieval times by tradesmen and craftsmen, a fact that has shaped its character to this day: narrow alleys and

Plaça de Sant Jaume: in the Palau de la Generalitat resides the Catalan government

archways, small, rather modest houses, workshops.

In the 1960s a start was made restoring the crumbling buildings. Today, the quarter is totally hip, by day and by night: small unusual shops, ateliers of fashion designers and other creative persons, galleries, trendy restaurants, pubs and cafés. Nevertheless, much of the authentic atmosphere has remained, and it is only a few paces to one of the city's most attractive parks, the *Parc de la Ciutadella*.

◼1 CARRER DE MONTCADA
(123 E4–5) (*Ø J 10*)

This well-preserved alley in the Ribera quarter is a true jewel of late medieval architecture. Within a small area you find here a unique ensemble of town palaces from the 14th century, Catalonia's heyday. Beautiful wooden gates and courtyards point to the wealth and taste of the aristocratic merchants who had these fine houses built. When the palaces threatened to disintegrate in the 1950s, they were bought up by the city and restored to perfection one by one. Today, most buildings house museums, galleries or exhibition centres. *Metro: Jaume I (L4)*

◼2 MUSEU PICASSO (PICASSO MUSEUM) ★ (123 E4) (*Ø J 10*)

The city's most visited museum mainly shows works from the early creative period of Pablo Picasso, the Blue Period, which coincides with his years in Barcelona. Living in the Catalan metropolis between 1895 and 1904, the painter was part of the artistic avant-garde and bohemian scene, and found first recognition. All his life he felt a strong tie to Barcelona, even during his exile in France during the

The Catalan parliament is at home in Parc de la Ciutadella

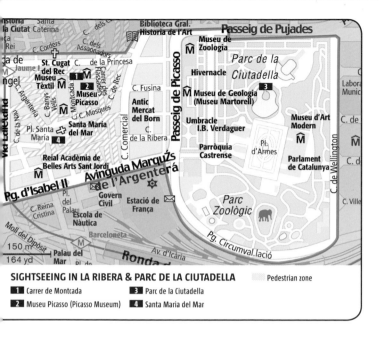

SIGHTSEEING IN LA RIBERA & PARC DE LA CIUTADELLA

■1 Carrer de Montcada   ■3 Parc de la Ciutadella

■2 Museu Picasso (Picasso Museum)   ■4 Santa Maria del Mar

▨ Pedestrian zone

Franco dictatorship. From the 1930s Picasso would donate paintings to the city, amongst them his famous Harlequin, but it was only in 1963 that the scattered works were united under one museum roof: on the initiative of a friend and secretary of Picasso's Jaume Sabartés, who also donated his comprehensive private collection. Initially housed in a Gothic palais on Carrer de Montcada, the museum today extends across five splendid residences. Bit by bit the collection was completed, Picasso gifting the museum his famous Menina series and all early works from the family's residence in Barcelona; his widow Jacqueline added valuable ceramics. Today, the museum represents the most important public Picasso collection alongside the one in Paris. *Tue–Sun 10am–8pm | admission 10 euros, changing exhibitions only 6 euros, free every first Sun of the month and every* *Sun 3–8pm | Montcada, 15 | www.museu picasso.bcn.es | Metro: Jaume I (L4)*

■3 PARC DE LA CIUTADELLA ●
(135 D–E 4–5) (*ⵍ K 9–10*)

Where today the park with its lake provides some peace and quiet, there once stood a citadel detested by the Catalans. Erected in 1715 by Philip V after his victorious siege of Barcelona, the fortification served as a feared prison for the subjugation of the rebellious Catalans. The latter did not rest until the citadel fell in 1878 and a park was established on the grounds. In 1888 then, the complex was turned into the site for the Universal Exhibition. At the main entrance of the park, a fairytale castle-like building with golden crenellations is the former exhibition restaurant *Castells dels Tres Dragons,* designed by architect Lluís Domènech i Montaner (today the *Museum of Zoology*).

Two more pavilions can be found alongside it. They were closed when this edition went into print, with no date set for reopening: the *Hivernacle,* an airy construction of crystal and cast iron, and next door the *Umbracle*, a kind of tropical greenhouse in the style of the 19th century. The centre of the park is the tall cascade with its extravagant sculpture, in which Gaudí was involved in as a student. At the lower end of the park lies *Barcelona Zoo (Nov–March daily 10am–5pm, March–mid-May and mid-Sept–Oct daily 10am–6pm, mid-May–mid-Sept daily 10am–7pm | admission 16.50 euros | www.zoobarcelona.com)*. Next to it stands the Catalan parliament. *Park March and Nov daily 10am–7pm, April and Oct daily 10am–8pm, May–Sept daily 10am–9pm, Dec–Feb daily 10am–6pm | Metro: Arc de Triomf (L1), Ciutadella (L4)*

◪ SANTA MARIA DEL MAR
(123 E5) (*∅ J 10*)

For many, this has to be the most beautiful church in Barcelona. Designed in pure Catalan Gothic style, the fascination of this church resides in its artful simplicity: no pomp nor circumstance disturbs the impression of space, openness and meditative silence. Skilfully designed polychrome stained-glass windows, partly from the 15th century, bathe the nearly empty nave (the choir stalls and furnishings burned in the Civil War) in INSIDERTIP near-mystical light, enhancing the impression of deep inner calm. The building with its high slender columns inside, was erected between 1329 and 1384 – record time for a big medieval church, which also helps to explain its stylistic uniformity. If you have the chance to attend a concert here, you can enjoy the INSIDERTIP extraordinary acoustics as well as the architecture. *Mon–Sat 9am–1.30pm and 4.30–8.30pm, Sun 10am–1.30pm and 4.30–8.45pm | Plaça de Santa María | Metro: Jaume I (L4)*

EIXAMPLE

The Eixample quarter was born in the 19th century as a residential quarter for the up-and-coming Catalan bourgeoisie. Work began in 1859 to designs by Ildefons Cerdà, a young progressive construction engineer. Cerdà was thinking of a revolutionary project in the American mould: a modern light-filled new town with a generously laid-out grid of streets centring around humankind. His designs however were only realised in a rather twisted version. What makes the quarter unique are its splendid buildings in Catalan Art Nouveau style. In the *Quadrat d'Or*, the Golden Square (south of Av. Diagonal, between Aribau and Sant Joan), over 150 buildings have been listed now, and they vie to surpass each other in beauty. The Eixample is much more than an Art Nouveau open-air museum: shops, galleries, restaurants, bars and street cafés in modern design make it one of the city's most vibrant quarters.

◪ CASA AMATLLER (134 C1) (*∅ J 8*)

Designed by Josep Puig i Cadafalch, this building (1898–1900) forms part of the famous block of houses on Passeig de Gràcia (between the streets of Consell de Cent and Aragó), locally called *Mançana de la Discòrdia*: 'apple of discord', i.e. bone of discontent. The name refers to the argument about which of these architectural wonders is the most beautiful (including Gaudí's Casa Batlló and Casa Lleó Morera by Lluís Domènech i Montaner). Casa Amatller shows how *modernisme* was inspired by neo-Gothic, Catalonia's 'golden era'. *Atrium freely*

Which building is prettier? Casa Amatller (left) or Casa Batlló (right)?

accessible during the day, daily 10am–8.30pm | guided tour (studio flat of Antoni Amatller) Wed at 12 noon in Spanish, Fri at 12 noon in English | guided tour 10 euros | Passeig de Gràcia, 41 | www.am attler.com | Metro: Passeig de Gràcia (L2, L3, L4)

2 CASA BATLLÓ ● (134 C1) (ØJ 8)
Modified by Antoni Gaudí between 1904 and 1906, the building forms part of the Mançana de la Discòrdia. For this fantastic piece of architecture, which was included in the Unesco World Heritage list in 2005, Gaudí again turned to nature for inspiration: the gently undulating façade is covered with shimmering mosaics; bizarre balconies and bays appear like bones or masks, stone columns like elephant's feet. The roof construction is reminiscent of a giant reptile – an allusion to the allegory of the dragon slayer Sant Jordi, the city's patron saint. Daily 9am–8pm (when events take place here only to 2pm) | admission 17.50 euros (incl. audio guide) | Passeig de Gràcia, 43 | www.casabatllo.es | Metro: Passeig de Gràcia (L2, L3, L4)

3 CASA LLEÓ MORERA
(134 C1) (ØJ 8)
The third building of the fantastic Mançana de la Discòrdia, designed by Lluís Domènech i Montaner (1902 to 1906). The décor has been skilfully worked in pure Art Nouveau style, with a sheer inexhaustible variety of floral elements, whether painted, in stone, plaster, glass, wood or ceramics. Not open to the public | Passeig de Gràcia, 35 | Metro: Passeig de Gràcia (L2, L3, L4)

4 CASA MILÀ/LA PEDRERA ★ ●
(128 C5) (ØJ 7)
Antoni Gaudí's most famous house is commonly known as La Pedrera, the quarry: a building hewn from stone without supporting walls, with massive undulating shapes on the façade, tree-trunks like pillars and undulating

balconies evoking plants. With this bold building, the architect let his exuberant imagination truly run riot. What is unique is the ☸ roof landscape (accessible to visitors) of chimneys and flues that sometimes appear like totems, sometimes helmeted soldiers – a precursor of the modern environment, with a panoramic view thrown in. In 1984, the building was declared a Unesco World Heritage site. What you can see are one flat, the roof terrace and the *Espai Gaudí* with multimedia information on the life and work of the master architect. The first floor shows changing art exhibitions. *March–Oct daily 9am–8pm, Nov–Feb daily 9am–6.30pm | admission 11 euros, changing exhibition on first floor free of charge | Passeig de Gràcia, 92 | www. fundaciocaixacatalunya.org | Metro: Diagonal (L3, L5)*

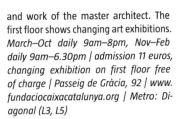

Wavy façade: Casa Milà, Gaudí's most famous house

5 CASA TERRADES/ CASA DE LES PUNXES
(129 D5) (Ø J 7)

Erected in 1905, the red-brick building designed by Josep Puig i Cadafalch combines north European Gothic with Catalan tradition. Its six pointed towers resembling witches' hats earned it the nickname *Casa de les Punxes* (House of the Spikes). The eccentric building seems to have been taken from the world of fairy-tales. *Interior not accessible to the public | Av. Diagonal, 416 | Metro: Diagonal (L3, L5)*

6 FUNDACIÓ TÀPIES (TÀPIES FOUNDATION) (128 C6) (Ø J 8)

In 1990, Antoni Tàpies, Catalonia's most important contemporary artist, opened his own museum. Built by Art Nouveau architect Lluís Domènech i Montaner, the building houses one of the most comprehensive collections of Tàpies works in the world. There are also changing exhibitions featuring international, often highly topical artists. *Tue–Sun 10am–7pm | admission 7 euros | Aragó, 255 | www. fundaciotapies.org | Metro: Passeig de Gràcia (L2, L3, L4)*

7 HOSPITAL DE SANT PAU
(130 A5) (Ø M 7)

In 1902 Lluís Domènech i Montaner designed a new city hospital that was revolutionary for the time. In order for the patients to recuperate better in the fresh air and in green spaces, he built 26

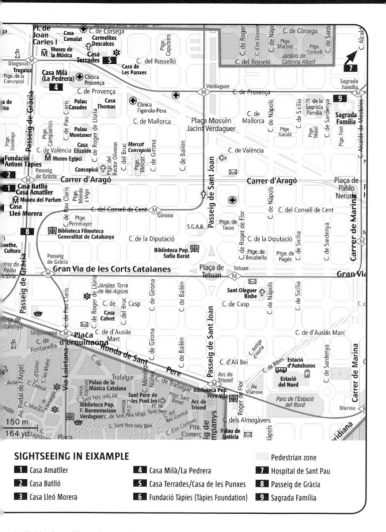

SIGHTSEEING IN EIXAMPLE

1 Casa Amatller
2 Casa Batlló
3 Casa Lleó Morera
4 Casa Milà/La Pedrera
5 Casa Terrades/Casa de les Punxes
6 Fundació Tàpies (Tàpies Foundation)

▨ Pedestrian zone

7 Hospital de Sant Pau
8 Passeig de Gràcia
9 Sagrada Família

individual pavilions in a park; connecting corridors and service offices were hidden underground. Domènech i Montaner equipped the pavilions with plenty of art and colours, believing in their healing powers. The ceramic-tiled roofs with their turrets and the entrance hall, adorned with ornate mosaics, are unique. Used as a hospital up to 2009 and following thorough restoration works, the complex is now accessible to the public as an arts centre. *Guided tours 10, 11, 12 noon and 1pm in English, 11.30am in Spanish | 10 euros | Sant Maria Claret, 167–171 | www. rutadelmodernisme.com | Metro: Hospital de Sant Pau (L5)*

8 PASSEIG DE GRÀCIA
(128 C5–6, 134 C1) (*M J 7–8*)

Swanky boulevard boasting magnificent Art Nouveau buildings and palaces, amongst them important monuments of *modernisme,* such as Gaudí's La Pedrera. At the same time an overview of the grand bourgeoisie's need for ostentation and prestige. Everybody who was anybody in 19th-century Barcelona built a residence or commercial premises on the Passeig de Gràcia. To this day, exclusive fashion shops, jewellers, luxury hotels and fancy restaurants cluster here – but also increasingly fast-food tapas bars.

9 SAGRADA FAMÍLIA ★ ●
(129 F5–6) (*M L 7*)

With its huge towers corkscrewing parabola-like into the sky, this temple of atonement dedicated to the Holy Family, originally commissioned by the arch-conservative Josephine congregation as a Catholic bulwark against the encroaching frivolous free spirit of the late 19th century, became a symbol of *modernisme* – and the world-famous emblem of Barcelona. Antoni Gaudí spent four decades of his life building his unfinished main work and testament, with the last twelve years of his life exclusively dedicated to this project. When he died in 1926, he had only completed the apse, one of the 18 planned towers, the neo-Gothic crypt and the eastern façade dedicated to the Birth of Christ (Christmas façade). This represented about a tenth of the complete work.

Since then, work has continued on this church of penitence, financed by donations and entrance fees. Ten thousand 'sinners' will be able to fit inside – once the building is finished one day. When this happens, a monumental, 557-ft tower reminiscent of a vertical airship is planned to crown the centre of the church.

Optimists reckon this will happen in 2026, for the centenary of Gaudí. By that stage a broad esplanade is scheduled to lead up to the planned main entrance in Carrer Mallorca – however, there are a few residential buildings in the way still. Meanwhile the church has been roofed, and in 2010 it was consecrated as a basilica by the Pope. The roof of the spectacular nave rests on gigantic columns straining skywards and projecting like trees into the space. A constant presence in Gaudí's work was the tree, which he called his most important source of inspiration. Upwards the columns branch out into funnel-like shapes, interspersed with shimmering trencadis, the broken tile shards used by Gaudí. The monumental backdrop makes humans appear tiny. Even critics of the continuation of the building works now admit to being impressed by the church interior – while the posthumously designed façades remain controversial. Le Corbusier, Gropius and Salvador Dalí were all against the continuation of work on Sagrada Família following Gaudí's death. To this day there are protests, in particular against the sculptures by Josep María Subirachs on the Passion Façade (northern side) – more kitsch than art, complain those opposed to the continuation, fearing that it's a 'Gaudílandia' that's being set up here, a theme park of attractions for the thousands of visitors that are corralled through the church on a daily basis. There is no way, they claim, of knowing how Gaudí would really have designed his church in the end, as he was constantly changing and improvising things on the site. Those in favour of the works say that the organic architecture of the Master followed geometric laws that have supposedly been decrypted and are now being implemented. Gaudí himself saw the mammoth temple in the tradition of medieval cathedrals, the completion of

The interior of Barcelona's icon, the Sagrada Família, is spectacular too

which took generations, once calling his work a 'sermon in stone'. Indeed, every single architectural element has been inspired by nature, religion and/or mysticism. To get up on the 🔍 towers you have to queue at the elevator; the stairs may only be used for coming back down. *April–Sept daily 9am–8pm, Oct–March daily 9am–6pm | admission 12.50 euros, with guided tour 16.50 euros, elevator 2.50 euros | Plaça de la Sagrada Família | www.sagradafamilia.org | Metro: Sagrada Família (L2, L5)*

RAVAL & RAMBLA

Up to the mid-18th century, the monasteries, gardens, hospitals and craft workers congregated outside the medieval city walls in Raval.

During industrialisation, factories and workers' lodgings sprang up here, until in the early 20th century the southern part of the quarter became known as the port and red-light district under the name of *Barri Xino*. However, in the 1990s the hotels-by-the hour and brothels had to make place for the modernisation of the quarter. Today, in Raval contrasts clash more visibly than anywhere else in Barcelona: crumbling alleyways rub shoulders with avant-garde galleries, hip bars and spit-and-sawdust places, lounge bars, luxury hotels, demi-monde establishments and historic buildings. There are long-established residents as well as immigrants, fashion designers, drug dealers and artists – a rich and creative microcosm with its own share of conflicts. In the wake of the quarter's renovation entire flights of streets were rebuilt, the Boulevard Rambla del Raval in particular, with its trendy bars and restaurants – not to be confused with Barcelona's famous boulevard of La Rambla. The latter forms the border between Raval and the Gothic Quarter.

■ ANTIC HOSPITAL DE LA SANTA CREU (134 B3) (*∅ H 10*)

This unique Gothic hospital complex, one of the oldest in existence, was begun in 1401 and served as the central hospital up to 1926; Barcelona's famous architect Antoni Gaudí died here too. Today, the building shelters the *Biblioteca de Catalunya* (not open to the public). Don't miss taking a look at the INSIDER TIP romantic inner courtyard with its orange trees – a visit is particularly recommended during the summer concert season. *Carrer del Carme, 47 | Metro: Liceu (L3)*

② CENTRE DE CULTURA CONTEMPORÀNIA (CENTRE FOR CONTEMPORARY CULTURE) (122 B2) (*∅ H 9*)

This is the thematic axis at the centre of the exhibitions, concerts, dance performances, photo and video art happenings in the city. The juxtaposition of old and new architecture is fascinating: the façade and courtyard are remnants of an orphanage (1802), which was complemented by a INSIDER TIP large-scale glass construction to make up a unique ensemble. *Tue, Wed and Fri–Sun 11am–8pm, Thu 11am–10pm | admission 5 euros, Thu 8–10pm and every first Sun of the month free of charge| Montalegre, 5 | www.cccb.org | Metro: Universitat (L1, L2)*

③ MUSEU D'ART CONTEMPORANI (MUSEUM OF CONTEMPORARY ART) (122 B2) (*∅ H 9*)

Bright white and flooded with light, elegant and Mediterranean: this avant-garde

Candy-coloured and totally hip: second-hand fashion in the creative trendy quarter of Raval

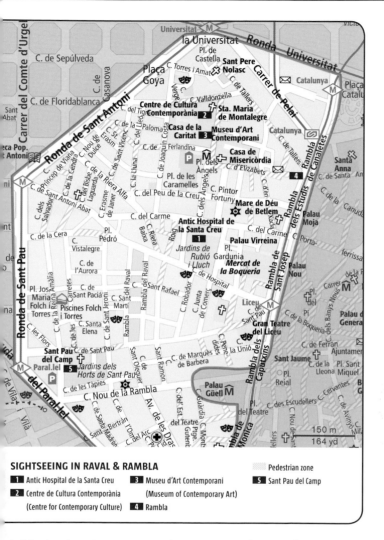

SIGHTSEEING IN RAVAL & RAMBLA

1 Antic Hospital de la Santa Creu

2 Centre de Cultura Contemporània
(Centre for Contemporary Culture)

3 Museu d'Art Contemporani
(Museum of Contemporary Art)

4 Rambla

5 Sant Pau del Camp

////// Pedestrian zone

building (1995) was designed by America's star architect Richard Meier. The museum shows interesting changing exhibitions. *24 June–24 Sept Mon and Wed–Fri 11am–8pm, Sat 10am–8pm, Sun 10am–3pm, 25 Sept–23 June Mon, Wed–Fri 11am–7.30pm, Sat 10am–8pm, Sun 10am–3pm | admis-sion 7.50 euros | Plaça dels Àngels, 1 | www.macba.es | Metro: Universitat (L1, L2)*

4 RAMBLA ★ ●

(122 C2–5) (*ω H 9–11*)

Even if the boulevard is only a bit over half a mile long: this short way between

Plaça de Catalunya and the port shows the different faces of the city, and you can feel the atmosphere and rhythm of the life, history and future of Barcelona. Ceaselessly populated by a colourful maelstrom of people: housewives and office workers, street musicians and opera-goers, prostitutes and pickpockets (be particularly careful in the human scrum!) – Las Ramblas are a stage and auditorium at the same time. Acrobatically skilled waiters balancing trays brave the thundering traffic at either side of the tree-lined promenade with its portrait painters, tarot-card readers and flower sellers. On the Rambla art exhibitions are organised, tourists fleeced and the victories of FC Barcelona celebrated. Historic buildings rub shoulders with both decrepit and luxurious hotels, modernist buildings and Art Nouveau shops with fast-food outlets and souvenir outlets.

Laid out in a dried-out riverbed, up to the 18th century the Rambla was actually outside the city walls. Monasteries and schools stood here. Only in the 19th century did the Rambla turn into a grand boulevard for Barcelona's upwardly mobile bourgeoisie to live and stroll on. Here the Civil War parties shot at each other, anarchists planted bombs, aristocrats attended the opera at the Liceu and afterwards the Meublés at the lower end of the Rambla – where small-time criminals and prostitutes still ply their trades today.

This promenade mirrors wonderfully the opposing character traits that make up the Catalan way of being, *seny* and *rauxa:* while the upper part (from Plaça de Catalunya looking towards the port) is more dominated by practical reason *(seny)*, in the lower part (looking in the direction of the port from Plaça del Teatre) the *rauxa* of unbridled passion gains the upper hand.

5 INSIDER TIP ▶ SANT PAU DEL CAMP
(122 A4) *(𝄞 G 10)*

The pretty little monastic ensemble on the edge of the Barri Xino was built in the 10th century on a green field and is now one of the few remaining Romanesque buildings in Barcelona. The church is plain and without aisles, the cloister with garden is endowed with an unadorned beauty – an oasis of calm amidst the big-city noise and bustle. *Mon–Sat 10am–1.15pm and 5–7.30pm | admission 3 euros | Carrer de Sant Pau, 101 | Metro: Parallel (L3)*

KEEP FIT!

Get to know the sights, history and culture running: a sports scientist and marathon runner founded *Sightjogging* to move Barcelona visitors through the city at a jog, accompanied by an experienced guide. There are seven different tours running between 6 and 10 in the morning, one of them again in the evening. The groups have no more than 4 people (from 35 euros for 60 minutes). The tours at sunrise or sunset are especially appealing. Book at least a day in advance under *www.sightjogging-barcelona.com or tel. 6 20 46 93 91.*

The beauty of simplicity: cloister in the Romanesque monastic complex of Sant Pau del Camp

BARCELONETA & OLD PORT

This quarter became famous as Barcelona's fishing village. With its narrow alleys and lines of washing extending between the houses, there are echoes of the old quarter of Naples.

In this quarter on the shores of the Mediterranean, established in 1753, fishermen, mariners and port workers once lived in light and sun-filled houses. With the decline of fishing and seafaring some hundred years ago, Barceloneta started going downhill.

In the course of the Olympic renewal, here too many houses were torn down and restored. The Old Port between Bar-

celoneta and Rambla was turned into a modern marina, the shabby industrial sheds made way for a new promenade lined with restaurants. Now, the *Moll de la Barceloneta* has long been one of the city's most popular leisure destinations and skateboard pistes. A few paces on, removed from the shore, the real Barceloneta starts, with crumbling façades and windows that see very little light. Neighbourhood life is still intact, but since the beach quarter close to the city centre has become fashionable, long-established tenants are increasingly turned out of their run-down flats, which are renovated to turn them into lucrative tourist apartments. Despite all this, you can still find a lot of the maritime charm of the old fishing village. The typical bars and restaurants where you can eat well for little money are still there; often they are the INSIDER TIP small, inconspicuous places that many pass without a second glance.

1 AQUÀRIUM ● (134 C5) (*J 11*)

Superb show of over 8000 animals and plants from all the world's oceans, with replica coral reefs, habitats and deep-sea scenarios. The biggest attraction of one of Europe's largest aquariums is an over 80-metre long transparent tunnel through which visitors pass below a gigantic ocean-arium, with sharks and other bizarre ocean dwellers swimming above their heads. *July and Aug daily 9.30am–11pm, Sept–June Mon–Fri 9.30am–9pm, Sat and Sun 9.30am–9.30pm | admission 17.75 euros | Moll d'Espanya del Port Vell | www.aquari-umbcn.com | Metro: Barceloneta (L4)*

2 MONUMENT A CRISTÓBAL COLOM (COLUMBUS MONUMENT) ☆

(122 B6) (*H 11*)

When Columbus returned from America in 1493, it was to a ceremonial reception in the port of Barcelona. The 195-ft mon-umental column in the Corinthian style was erected in 1888 for the World Exhi-bition. The viewing platform gives you a fantastic view over the harbour and the old town. *Daily 8.30am–8.30pm | admission 3 euros | Plaça del Portal de la Pau | Metro: Drassanes (L3)*

3 MUSEU MARÍTIM (MARITIME MUSEUM)

(122 B6) (*H 11*)

The museum is housed in the *Drassanes*, one of the largest and most beautiful medieval shipping docks in the world. Established in the 13th and 14th centu-ries, the dock allowed for up to 30 ves-sels to be built at the same time. Today, the story of Catalonia's shipping history is told here. On show are imposing repli-cas of important ships, partly in original size, in the case of the replica of a 60m-long galley, plus original ship models, nautical instruments and figureheads. For renovation works, up to 2013 prob-ably, only parts of the museum are open to visitors. *Daily 10am–7pm | admission 2.50 euros, Sun from 3pm free of charge*

Amble past sharks: there's no danger in the see-through tunnel of one of Europe's largest aquariums

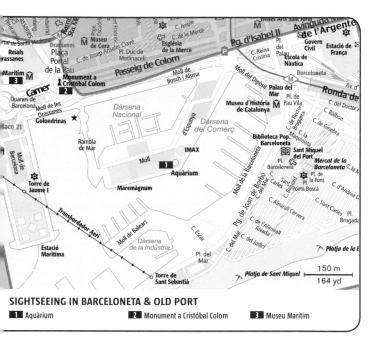

SIGHTSEEING IN BARCELONETA & OLD PORT

1 Aquàrium   **2** Monument a Cristóbal Colom   **3** Museu Marítim

| Av. Drassanes, 1 | www.diba.es/mma ritim | Metro: Drassanes (L3)

OTHER CITY QUARTERS

GRÀCIA

(128–129 B–E 2–5) (*m* J–K 5–7)

This cosy part of town beyond Diagonal and Passeig de Gràcia has much neighbourhood feeling. You'll still feel a bit of the tranquillity of the village that Gràcia used to be before its incorporation into Big Barcelona: small houses and craft workshop, little bars and restaurants, corner shops and street cafés, squares, patios and terraces wherever you go.

Amongst the most beautiful squares of the district are ● **INSIDER TIP** *Plaça de la Vila* and *Plaça de la Virreina*. In the 1970s, Barcelona's alternative arts movement started from Gràcia. Today still, many small theatres, hip restaurants and bars, galleries and alternative shops remain – even thought the avant-garde is now happening more in Raval and Ribera. *Metro: Fontana (L3), FGC: Gràcia*

OLYMPIC PORT, BEACH & FORUM
(136–137 A–F 5–6) (*Ⓜ L–Q 11*)

The urban renewal for the Olympic Games of 1992 also brought the city attractive beaches that extend northwards from Barceloneta to the Olympic village *(Vila Olímpica)* with its modern marina. The ● mile-long sandy beach is not only suitable for swimming; you can also walk the entire stretch of palm-fringed promenade where benches and bars beckon for a relaxing break at any time of the year. Visible from Barceloneta, the futuristic building of the gas works, inaugurated in 2006, was designed by star architect Enric Miralles (1955–2000) and Benedetta Tagliabue. Frank O. Gehry contributed a fascinating large-scale sculpture – an almost 50-metre-long bronze fish, whose aspect changes depending on the angle

of the sun. The sculpture stands on the beach in front of the 'twin towers' of the Olympic village: the *Arts* luxury hotel and an award-winning office tower. While there is a profusion of restaurants, stalls and bars on this stretch of beach, it gets calmer the further northwards you go. Balmy summer nights bring out Barcelona's night owls to the pretty beach bars (at the weekends in particular) with parties, live music, DJs and drinks, to lounge on deckchairs or sofas with a view of the sea.

Along the diagonal between Plaça de les Glòries and the area of the Forum *(Diagonal Mar),* imposing office and hotel towers designed by architects such as David Chipperfield and Dominique Perrault rise into the Mediterranean sky.

The colourful shimmering cigar-shaped high-rise, the 465 ft *Torre Agbar*, was commissioned by the waterworks and designed by the French architect Jean Nouvel. Since 2004 the building has crowned the postmodern skyline of the coastal strip. Enric Miralles and Bened-

RELAX & ENJOY

For a relaxing short massage after hours of treading the cobbles, try ● *Masajes a 1000* studio, a few paces off the fancy boulevard of Passeig de Gràcia *(daily 8am–11pm, with or without reservations | 5 min 4.60 euros, 20 minutes 18.40 euros | Mallorca, 233 | tel. 9 32 15 85 85 | Metro: Passeig de Gràcia (L2, L3, L4).*

Enjoy the exclusive baths and treatments of the in-house spa at the *Omm* design hotel, with sauna, ice or hammam showers, baths, pool, gym, aromatherapy, a range of massages

from Ayurvedic via classic to Balinese, and a hair salon *(Mon–Sat 9am–10pm, Sun 10am–6pm | Rosseló, 265 | tel. 9 34 45 49 49 | www.hotelomm.es | Metro: Diagonal (L3, L5).* Or flee the big-city stress in a futuristic floating capsule: the water contains such a high concentration of salt that your body floats as if free of the effects of gravity, relaxing muscles and the soul (● *Flotarium | daily 10am–10pm | from 35 euros | www.flotarium.com | Metro: Diagonal (L2, L3).*

etta Tagliabue designed the eccentrically playful *Parc Diagonal Mar (corner of Av. Diagonal and Taulat)* in the area of the Forum. Also in 2004, Swiss architects Jacques Herzog & Pierre de Meuron left their mark with the bright-blue auditorium and exhibition building *Edifici Fòrum*, which has won several awards. Together with the *congress hall* opposite (MAP Architects, also 2004) it forms one of the biggest congress and events ensembles in Europe, holding over 18,000 visitors. The most recent architectural eye-catcher is a 360ft avant-garde skyscraper right by the Forum area. The *Torre Diagonal Zero Zero (Torre Telefonica)* was designed by the young Catalan architect Enric Massip-Bosch for the Spanish telephone provider.

SANT PERE & SANTA CATERINA
(123 E–F 3–4) (*ﾉﾉ J–K 9–10*)

In the 12th and 13th centuries, craftsmen and traders made the 'twin quarters' between the streets of Via Laietana, Princesa and Sant Pere més alt into the flourishing centre of Barcelona. Later, Catalonia's first cloth factories would be established here. In their wake, workers and immigrants moved into the quarter; to this day, over half the population were born elsewhere.

A few years ago the urban renewal of these crumbling quarters started, first around the historic market hall of Santa Caterina, which was renovated and given a spectacular roof construction by architect Enric Miralles (died in 2000). The surrounding alleys have seen the opening of fashionable restaurants, galleries, chill-out bars or boutiques. Despite all this, Sant Pere and Santa Caterina still enchant visitors with their medieval ambience of winding little passages and charming squares.

Particularly attractive is INSIDER TIP *Plaça Sant Augustí Vell*, reminiscent of old Paris

Dazzling: Torre Agbar

with its historic façades and cast-iron lanterns. If you need to sit down, head for the tranquil INSIDER TIP *Plaça de Sant Pere* with its Romanesque church of *Sant Pere de Puelles*, an Art Nouveau fountain and façades ranging from medieval to modern.

SIGHTS IN OTHER QUARTERS

CAIXA FORUM ● (133 D2) (*⌖ E 9*)

The La Caixa foundation possesses one of Europe's most important collections of contemporary art. Over 800 works (from Joseph Beuys via Julian Schnabel to Sue Williams) are presented in the spectacularly restored *Casaramona* textile factory, an imposing Art Nouveau building by Josep Puig i Cadafalch. There are also interesting changing exhibitions and cultural events. *Sun–Fri 10am–8pm, Sat 10am–10pm | free admission | Av. Marquès de Comillas, 6–8 | www. fundacio.lacaixa.es | Metro: Espanya (L1, L3)*

COSMOCAIXA (SCIENCE MUSEUM) ●
(125 F3) (*⌖ H 3*)

Following expansion works lasting several years, this interactive science museum, one of the largest, most modern and innovative of its kind in Europe, has reopened. The idea is to experience science by experimenting and using your senses, from the formation of matter and life all the way to current ecosystems. Watch tropical rain drum down on crocodiles in the replicated Amazon jungle. Children in particular will love this museum. *Tue–Sun 10am–8pm | admission 3 euros, free on the first Sun in the month | Teodor Roviralta, 55 | www. fundacio.lacaixa.es | by suburban train FGC to Avinguda Tibidabo, then Tramvía Blau or on foot*

Fundació Joan Miró: Catalan art in the beautiful museum on Montjuïc

CEMENTIRI MONTJUÏC (MONTJUÏC CEMETERY)
(132 A–B 5) (*C–D 11*)

A stroll across Barcelona's most beautiful cemetery is like a voyage into the history of the city and its inhabitants. High above the city, the upwardly mobile bourgeoisie of the 19th century made themselves an ostentatious monument filled with magnificent pantheons and ornate chapels. At a safe distance lie the simple niche graves of the poor. Prominent artists such as Barcelona-born painter Joan Miró or the famous anarchist Buenaventura Durruti found their last resting place on Montjuïc. The dead, local wisdom has it, have a much better view from up here than many who are still alive. *Daily 8am–6pm | Mare de Déu de Port | www.cbsa.es | Metro: Espanya*

(*L1, L3*), on with bus no. 21, stop: Pg. Cementiri del Sud-Oest

FUNDACIÓ JOAN MIRÓ (JOAN MIRÓ FOUNDATION) ★
(133 D–E4) (*F 10*)

The artist himself set up the foundation in 1975. His friend Josep Lluís Sert, one of the leading Spanish architects of modern times, designed a uniquely beautiful museum on the Montjuïc. An open, light-filled, very Mediterranean construction with patios and terraces in a harmonious relation to the landscape provides the ideal framework for bringing out the beauty of works by Joan Miró (1893–1983). Get an overview of the creative trajectory of the great Catalan avant-garde painter, who became one of the most famous artists of the 20th century: from his first drawings in 1901 to his very last monumental paintings. The permanent collection also displays graphic art, wall hangings, ceramics and sculptures, plus changing exhibitions of modern and contemporary art. The bookshop and cafeteria are also recommended! *July–Sept Tue–Sat 10am–8pm, Oct–June Tue–Sat 10am–7pm, Thu all year round to 9.30pm, Sun all year round 10am–2.30pm | admission 9 euros | Parc de Montjuïc | www.fundaciomiro-bcn.org | Metro: Parallel (L2, L3), then by funicular to Montjuïc, or Espanya (L1, L3), on by foot or bus no. 50 and 55*

MONTJUÏC
(132–133 B–E 2–5) (*D–F 9–11*)

At a height of 567 ft, Barcelona's local mountain forms an integral part of the city's history, culture and leisure. When the Castilians laid siege to the city, they used the fortification complex on the summit, erected in the 17th century (today the military museum), in order to dominate the city. During the Franco

Arty break: the Palau Nacional harbours masterpieces of the Museum of Catalan Art

dictatorship still, the fortification was a feared prison. Today, the mountain is amongst Barcelona's most attractive recreation areas. The changes began with the 1929 World Exhibition, while the Olympic Games of 1992 brought the complete opening up of the area. Today, there are many attractions in the large grounds (see walk p. 99).

MUSEU NACIONAL D'ART DE CATALUNYA (MUSEUM OF CATALAN ART) ● (133 D3) (*Ø E 10*)

Find all of Catalonia's art under one roof. The collection of Romanesque art is considered unique in the world. Highlights are the colourful Romanesque frescoes. Taken from churches and chapels in the Catalan Pyrenees threatened with collapse, they are today presented in true-to-original replicated apses and altar niches – which brings out the simple beauty of these masterpieces even better. The collection of Gothic art is impressive too. Last not least you can enjoy exhibits from Renaissance and Baroque times, work by the Catalan modernists of the late 19th and early 20th century, or modern and contemporary art. Also on display is part of the private Thyssen-Bornemisza collection, providing a unique overview of European art from the Middle Ages to Venetian Late Baroque.

Schedule at least three hours for a visit to this mega-museum: you won't be sorry! *Tue–Sat 10am–7pm, Sun 10am–2.30pm | admission 8.50 euros incl. audio guide (valid for two days), free on the first Sun of the month | www.mnac.es | Metro: Espanya (L1, L3)*

INSIDER TIP ▶ MUSEU-MONESTIR PEDRALBES (124 A4) (*ᗰ E 3*)

This monastic complex is a gem of Gothic architecture. Inside you'll find medieval furniture, paintings and sculptures. The enchanting two-storey cloister is adorned with 14th-century wall paintings. *Oct–March Tue–Sat 10am–2pm, Sun 10am–8pm, April–Sept Tue–Sat 10am–5pm, Sun 10am–8pm | admission 7 euros (incl. admission Museu d'Història de la Ciutat), Sun free from 3pm | Baixada Monestir, 9 | www.museohistoria.bcn.es | FGC: Reina Elisenda*

INSIDER TIP ▶ PARC DEL LABERINT (0) (*ᗰ N 1*)

The neo-Classical gardens are a late 18th-century masterpiece laid out by their owner, the Marquis of Alfarràs. Time and again the visitor is surprised by playful Amor statues, water cascades, bridges, fountains and lakes, as well as small marble temples – a neo-Classical ensemble based on Italian models. While the park could do with a bit more upkeep these days, its decadent charm is still enchanting. The pretty, naive-arabesque palace of the Marquis at the centre features modernist elements. Why not get gently lost in the maze of cypress hedges... *March, Oct daily 10am–7pm, April daily 10am–8pm, May–Sept daily 10am–9pm, Nov–Feb daily 10am–6pm | admission 2 euros, Sun and Wed free | Metro: Mundet (L3)*

PARC GÜELL ★ ☼ ●
(129 E1) (*ᗰ K 4*)

Fairy-tale houses, dragon figures, gigantic grottoes, arcades rammed at an angle against the mountain: the picturesque park laid out by Antoni Gaudí above the city (1900–1911), which delighted Salvador Dalí, was placed under Unesco World Heritage protection in 1984. Gaudí's innovative work by, a commission by his patron Eusebi Güell, was originally planned as a spacious residential colony; however, only three houses were realised. Dominated by organic forms and natural materials, the complex serves

LOW BUDGET

▶ ● Students and master pupils of the Catalan conservatory give regular evening concerts – usually free of charge. *Escola Superior de Música de Catalunya | (135 F2) (ᗰ L 9) Padilla, 155 | tel. 9 33 52 30 11 | www.esmuc. cat | Metro: Glòries (L1)*

▶ Current art trends are on show at *La Capella (Tue–Sat 12 noon–2pm and 4–8pm, Sun 11am–2pm | (122 B3) (ᗰ H 10) Hospital 56 | Metro: Liceu (L3)*. Also free of charge are the exhibitions at the *Arts Santa Mònica (122 B5) (ᗰ H 11)*, a former 18th-century monastery on the Rambla *(Tue–Sun 11am–9pm | La Rambla, 7 | www.artssantamonica.cat | Metro: Drassanes (L3)*.

▶ At the popular shows *(funciones populares)* put on by the *Gran Teatre del Liceu (www.liceubarcelona.com)* you hear opera sung by emerging talents at discounts of up to 50 per cent. Everybody under 26 and over 65 also benefits from a 30 per cent discount for last-minute tickets.

▶ ● A number of museums, amongst them the *Museu Picasso* and the *Museu d'Història*, offer free admission on some Sundays or on every Sunday afternoon.

as an illustration found nowhere else of Gaudí's universal genius as architect, artist, craftsman and landscape planner. At the park's centre, a huge terrace (originally planned as a market) is supported by Doric columns, forming a bizarre hall below. A long curvy stone bench snakes

A colourful dragon: friendly guard in Parc Guëll

its way across the terrace, which affords breathtaking panoramic views. Like many works by Gaudí it was made in the trencadis method, a collage technique yielding colourful mosaics from glass and pottery shards.

Symbolic motifs and sculptures can be discovered everywhere, at the entrance to the staircase for instance the luminous dragon Python, who according to Greek legend guards the subterranean waters. The park is a unique, happy combination of architecture and nature. Gaudí took care to be economical and ecological in his constructions, using materials found in the grounds. For his mosaics he used what the neighbouring ceramics factories were throwing away: if you look carefully at the ceiling rosettes, you can make out the undersides of plates or cup handles. And through the inside of the Doric columns rainwater flows into the underground reservoir. The grounds also hold the *Gaudí Museum* in the former residence of the master, with mementoes of his life. *March and Nov daily 10am–7pm, April and Sept daily 10am–8pm, May–Aug daily 10am–9pm, Nov–Feb daily 10am–6pm | Carrer d'Olot | Metro: Lesseps (L3), Alfonso X (L4)*

TIBIDABO ☀ (125 E1–2) (*⑪ H–J 1–2*)
At 1640 ft this is the city's highest point. The trip up in the open tram carriages of Tramvía Blau *(from Av. del Tibidabo | 24 June–11 Nov daily 10am–8pm, outside those times Sat and Sun 10am–6pm)* through Barcelona's fancy quarter is an experience. At the final stop panorama bars and a garden restaurant await, while a funicular can take you all the way up to the summit – and a funfair with Ferris wheel and carousels, as well as the TV tower. *March–Dec, spring and autumn only Sat and Sun | admission to fun park 25.20 euros | variable opening times |*

tel. 9 32 11 79 42 | www.tibidabo.es | FGC: Tibidabo, then Tramvía Blau and funicular or bus no. 196

TORRE DE COLLSEROLA (TV TOWER) 🌿 (0) (🅼 0)

Erected for the 1992 Olympic Games, the TV tower on the Tibidabo is a work of Norman Foster. From up here you have a fabulous 360-degree view (on a clear day for over 40 miles) beyond the city. A glass elevator whisks you at breathtaking speed to the viewing platform at a height of 377 ft. *Oct–Dec and March/April Sat and Sun 12 noon–2pm and 3.30–6pm, May Sat and Sun 12 noon–2pm and 3.30–7pm, June Sat and Sun 11am–2pm and 3.30–5pm, July/Aug Wed–Sun 12 noon–2pm and 5.30–8pm | admission 5 euros | www.torredecollserola.com | suburban train (FGC) S1, S2 to Peu de Funicular, then Funicular Vallvidrera*

OUTSIDE THE CITY

ABADIA DE MONTSERRAT
(138 C4) (🅼 0)

The very popular Benedictine monastery of Montserrat shelters the *Moreneta* (black Madonna), the patron saint of Catalonia. Founded around the year 880,

BOOKS & FILMS

▶ **The City of Marvels** – Eduardo Mendoza's colourful brilliantly satirical novel is set between 1888 and 1929 and tells the story of the adventurous rise of a young architect to become the most powerful man in Barcelona.

▶ **Thrillers by Manuel Vázquez Montalbán** – Private eye, gourmet and cynic Pepe Carvalho fights crime and corruption in the brave new Barcelona in his own way.

▶ **The Shadow of the Wind** – In his bestselling many-layered novel, Carlos Ruiz Zafón captures the charm of Barcelona, with heavy Gothic touches.

▶ **Barcelona** – Robert Hughes' evocation of the city is one of the classics of modern travel writing; the condensed version is called Barcelona: The Great Enchantress.

▶ **Cathedral of the Sea** – The story of life in medieval Barcelona and the construction of the Santa Maria del Mar cathedral is told by Ildefonso Falcone in his 2006 novel which became an international bestseller.

▶ **All About my Mother** – Pedro Almodóvar's Oscar-winning melodrama (1999) about love and the seemingly unbending strength of women is one of the best films by the Spanish star director.

▶ **Vicky Cristina Barcelona** – The Catalan metropolis inspired Woody Allen in 2008 to a nimble comedy around the trials and tribulations of love. Featuring Scarlett Johansson, Javier Bardem and Penélope Cruz, who received an Oscar for her supporting role.

the complex stands on a bizarrely jagged rock formation – the fantastic natural backdrop making up for the touristy infrastructure of restaurants and souvenir shops. Don't miss the Gregorian chants intoned at lunchtime by 50 choirboys *(Mon–Fri 1pm, Sun 12 noon). Monastery daily 9am–8pm, in winter 9am–5.45pm, Black Madonna 7–10.30am and 12 noon–6.30pm, July–Sept also 7.30–8.15pm | free admission | www.abadiamontserrat. net | motorway A2, exit Martorell, then national road NII (approx. 37 mi northwest of Barcelona), or suburban train FGC from Plaça Espanya (approx. 1 hr one way) to Monestrol de Montserrat, then change to the funicular (approx. 15 min.)*

INSIDER TIP CRIPTA DE LA COLONIA GÜELL (0) (*W O*)

Even though only the crypt of the planned church is visible, this fragment is amongst Antoni Gaudí's masterpieces. Many even hold the fantastical and complex crypt, which makes do with nearly no right angles, to be his most daring and modern project. The incomplete church stands at the centre of the Modernist workers' colony and factory complex Colonia Güell founded by textile magnate Eusebio Güell. *May–Oct Mon–Fri 10am–2pm and 3–7pm, Sat and Sun 10am–3pm, Nov–April daily 10am–3pm | admission 5 euros | Santa Coloma de Cervelló | FGC lines S3, S4, S7 from Plaça Espanya to Colonia Güell*

MONESTIR DE SANTES CREUS
(138 A5) (*W O*)

An oasis of calm awaits you in the Cistercian monastery of Monestir de Santes Creus, founded in 1158 and one of Catalonia's most beautiful monasteries. *June–Sept Tue–Sun 10am–6.30pm, Oct–May Tue–Sun 10am–5pm | admission 4.50 euros, Tue free | A2, exit Valls Vilarodona, approx. 1 hour's drive*

MONESTIR SANTA MARÍA DE POBLET
(138 A5) (*W O*)

Some 62 miles from Barcelona, Monestir Santa María de Poblet is one of Spain's most important monasteries and a UNESCO World Heritage site. The fortification walls shelter an entire monastic town. *Guided tours every 30 minutes, Mon–Sat 10am–12.40pm and 3–5.55pm, Sun 10am–12.25pm and 3–5.25pm |*

The Benedictine monastery of Montserrat lies amongst bizarrely jagged rocks

www.poblet.cat | admission 7 euros | A2, exit Montblanc, or train from Sants railway station in the direction of Lleida to L'Espluga de Francoli (approx. 2.5 mi from the monastery)

PENEDÉS (138 B5) (*ⓜ O*)

With its rolling hills, the charming wine-growing area of Penedés is reminiscent of Tuscany. A number of the excellent cellars of the region are open to the public, most of them around the villages of Sant Sadurni d'Anoia and Vilafranca. Some of the most interesting are the *Caves Codorníu (www.codorniu.es)* in Vilafranca, designed by Art Nouveau architect Josep Puig I Cadafalch. *Train from Sants railway station or by car on the A7*

SITGES (138 B6) (*ⓜ O*)

Pretty beaches and curious museums are the attractions of the resort of Sitges, approx. 25 miles south of Barcelona, with its luminous white houses, narrow lanes and fin-de-siècle charm: Sitges was a well-known artists' colony in the late 19th century. Today, this is also where the heart of Catalonia's thriving gay culture beats. From Sants station there are regular rail connections along the coast (approx. 30 min journey time). *By car A16*

TEATRE-MUSEU DALÍ ⭐
(139 F2) (*ⓜ O*)

A trip to Figueres to the Teatre-Museu Dalí, one of Spain's most-visited museums, is an unforgettable experience – not only for Dalí fans. The world-famous artist and eccentric Salvador Dalí created his own monument in the former theatre – a gigantic work of art. Crowned by concrete eggs, the building shelters the entire phantasmagorical universe of the surrealist icon. *July–Sept daily 9am–7.15pm, Oct and March–May Tue–Sun 9.30am–5.15pm, Nov–Feb Tue–Sun*

A mega-work in the Teatre-Museu Dalí

10.30am–5.15pm, June daily 9.30am–5.15pm, INSIDER TIP *in August also 10pm–1am by previous arrangement through www.salvador-dali.org | admission 12 euros | A7 north (ca. 87 mi from Barcelona) or train from Sants railway station (ca. 2 hours one way)*

FOOD & DRINK

Allowing the culinary pleasures of Catalonia to melt in your mouth not only gets you closer to the taste, but also to the country and its people.

The Catalans' food mirrors their contradictory character, always oscillating between *seny* and *rauxa*, between balancing reason and eruptive imagination. Taste the country in its strangely delicious combinations of sweet and spicy, fish and meat, that are called *mar i muntanya*, sea and mountain. Hearty stews and specialities made with sausage, game, forest mushrooms, lamb or pulses tend to originate from the interior. The dishes of the coastal region are lighter, particularly owing to the range of fresh fish and seafood.

The talent of magicking simple ingredients into imaginative dishes is a characteristic of Catalan cuisine – considered the best in Spain alongside Basque food. In Sant Pol de Mar near Barcelona stands the restaurant of Carme Ruscalleda, one of the few female chefs world-wide to be awarded three Michelin stars. Don't waste your time in one of the many fast-food outlets. There are other places where you can eat well for little money. Countless eateries and bars offer a daily **INSIDER TIP** good-value lunch menu, the *menú del día*: starter, main and dessert from 9 euros, often including a drink. At under 30 euros at lunchtime, even the culinary art of the gourmet restaurants is accessible.

Photo: Fish dish in the Gaig restaurant

Palate pleasers and conviviality: the Catalans love to enjoy good food and culinary fusion

The Catalans eat late: in the evening from about 9pm, at lunchtime not before 2pm – warm each time, with two courses and dessert. This relegates breakfast to a modest affair of a milky coffee and a *croissant* (the Spanish variety, not quite as refined), eaten in a hurry in the nearest *bar*. Depending on the time of day, these *bars* serve as café, snack bar, restaurant or pub. They function a bit like big living rooms, where part of daily life is played out.

At many restaurants you should reserve a table, on a Friday or Saturday in particular. On Sundays and public holidays, many restaurants close in the evenings, in July and August sometimes entirely (for one to three weeks). Make sure you call ahead during this time! Most restaurants open at lunchtime between about 1 and 4pm and in the evening between around 9pm and midnight. Many popular eateries are located in the Old Town: in the evenings, better take a taxi!

BARS, CAFÉS, TAVERNS & TAPAS BARS

Els Quatre Gats: a legendary artists' haunt 'the four tomcats' frequented by Picasso

BARS, CAFÉS, TAVERNS & TAPAS BARS

Granges is the name for the traditional milk bars selling hot chocolate, coffee and fresh pastries. Cafés are often open from morning to late at night and offer savoury as well as sweet snacks.

INSIDER TIP ▸ BAR DE L'ANTIC TEATRE
(123 E3) (*Ø J 9*)

This enchanting courtyard café with wooden benches and bohemian atmosphere in a 19th-century theatre is only a few paces from the Palau de la Música Catalana concert hall. *From 4pm, closed Sun | Verdaguer I Callís, 12 | Metro: Urquinaona (L4)*

BAR DEL CONVENT (123 F4) (*Ø K 10*)
Pretty little café under arcades, hidden away in the cloister of the Sant Au-gustí monastery. *Closed Sun | Plaça de l'Acadèmia | Metro: Jaume I (L4) or Arc de Triomf (L1)*

BAR LA PLATA (134 C4) (*Ø J 11*)
This small rustic bar with ceramic tiles and formica tables is frequented by both local residents and tourists looking for authentic ambience. You won't break the bank here: glasses of wine start at 1 euro. *Closed Sun and Aug | Mercé, 28 | Metro: Jaume I (L4)*

INSIDER TIP ▸ BAR MUNDIAL
(123 F4) (*Ø K 10*)

This authentic tapas bar has been around since 1908. The establishment on one of the prettiest squares in the Old Town has a familiar ambience. Fish and seafood a speciality. *Closed Sun evening, Tue lunchtime and Mon | Plaça Sant Augustí, 1 | Metro: Jaume I (L4)*

BODEGA L'ELECTRICITAT
(135 D6) (*ⓜ K 12*)
For over a hundred years an institution in the fishing village of Barceloneta! Wine and vermouth flow from large barrels on the wall. The neon lighting doesn't detract from the noisy and good-humoured atmosphere. *Tue–Sat 8am–3pm and 7–10.30pm | Sant Carles, 15 | Metro: Barceloneta (L4)*

CAN MARGARIT
(133 E3) (*ⓜ F 10*)
This cosy tavern is housed in a former stables. Simple dishes, great atmosphere – which explains why it's usually jam-packed. *Mon–Sat 9am–11.30pm | Concòrdia, 21 | tel. 9 34 41 67 23 | Metro: Poble Sec (L3)*

CERVECERIA CATALANA
(128 B6) (*ⓜ H 8*)
Popular bar classic: mountains of mouth-watering tapas around the clock at adequate prices. *Daily | Mallorca, 236 | Metro: Diagonal (L3, L5)*

INSIDER TIP ELS FOGONS DE LA BARCELONETA
(135 D5) (*ⓜ K 11*)
Modern tapas bar in the Santa Caterina market hall of Barceloneta. Ángel Pascual works her magic in the open-plan kitchen: snacks from classic to contemporary, from grilled sardines to pumpkin cream in three different textures and cod with liquorice. *Closed Sun evening and Mon | Plaça de la Font | tel. 9 32 24 26 26 | Metro: Barceloneta (L4)*

ELS QUATRE GATS
(123 D3) (*ⓜ J 9*)
Legendary artists' haunt with an Art Nouveau ambience, where Picasso and the Catalan bohème were regulars. Traditional Catalan cooking. *Closed Aug | Montsió, 5 | tel. 9 33 02 41 40 | Metro: Catalunya (L1, L3)*

EL XAMPANYET
(123 E5) (*ⓜ J 10*)
This rustic champagne bar serves *cavas*, wines and tasty tapas. An institution. *Closed Sun and Mon, as well as in Aug | Montcada, 22 | tel. 9 33 19 70 03 | Metro: Jaume I (L4)*

GRANJA VIADER
(122 C3) (*ⓜ H 10*)
Barcelona's oldest milk bar serves delicious cheesecake and *orxata* (almond milk). *Mon 5–8.30pm, Tue–Sat 9am–1pm and 5–8.30pm | Xuclà, 4 | Metro: Liceu (L3)*

INSIDER TIP TAPAS,24
(134 C1) (*ⓜ J 8*)
Star-garlanded chef Carles Abellán, well known for his mastery of experimental tapas, offers the classic version of these traditional snacks – in first-class quality. *Closed Sun | Diputació, 269 | tel. 9 34 88 09 77 | www.carlesabellan.com | Metro: Passeig de Gràcia (L3)*

★ **Hofmann**
This is where Barcelona's top chefs learn their trade → **p. 64**

★ **Mercat de la Boqueria**
Culinary meeting point in the Boqueria market hall → **p. 67**

★ **Gaig**
Haute cuisine with contemporary touches → **p. 62**

★ **Neichel**
Master of Mediterranean cuisine → **p. 62**

★ **Cal Pep**
Fabulous fish tapas → **p. 65**

MARCO POLO HIGHLIGHTS

TEXTIL CAFÉ (123 E4) (*Ⓜ J 10*)
A lovely café in the medieval patio of the textile museum that serves cakes and little snacks, as well as a lunch menu. *Closed Mon | Montcada, 12–14 | Metro: Jaume I (L4)*p

TRAVEL BAR
(134 B3) (*Ⓜ H 10*)
Information, contacts and tips for budget travellers. Around 8pm the Eurodinner arrives: order a drink and receive a homemade dish of the day for 1 euro. *Daily | Boqueria, 27 | www.travelbar.com | Metro: Liceu (L3)*

VELÓDROMO (128 A4) (*Ⓜ H 7*)
1930s café with bohemian flair, overseen by star chef Carles Abellán. Tapas menu. *Daily | Muntaner, 213 | Metro: Hospital Clinic (L5)*

ALKIMIA
(129 E5) (*Ⓜ K 7*)
Finest new Catalan cuisine, Michelin-starred: Jordi Vila is a virtuoso at playing with taste and texture – turning traditional tomato bread into a shot of white tomato juice, topped with olive

GOURMET RESTAURANTS

Drolma (128 C6) (*Ⓜ J 8*)
Exquisite Michelin-starred restaurant at the fancy Majestic hotel. Chef Fermí Puig spoils his guests with creative signature cuisine at the highest level, serving Mediterranean dishes with a French accent. The décor is classic with post-modern details. Even the service reaches heights of perfection. *Menu from 95 euros | closed Sun | Passeig de Gràcia, 70 | tel. 9 34 96 77 10 | Metro: Passeig de Gràcia (L2, L3, L4)*

Gaig ★ (128 B6) (*Ⓜ H 8*)
Top chef Carles Gaig, proud bearer of a Michelin star, combines a family tradition going back over 100 years with up-to-date haute cuisine. His innovative variations on Catalan cuisine are a culinary experience. Excellent wine list and cigar selection. *Menu from 85 euros | closed Sun and Mon | Aragó, 214 | in Hotel Cram | tel. 9 34 29 10 17 | www. restaurantgaig.com | Metro: Passeig de Gràcia (L2, L3, L4)*

Neichel ★ (126 C2) (*Ⓜ E 5*)
Independent of gastronomic fashions, Alsace-born chef Jean Louis Neichel presents his Michelin-starred cuisine as a happy combination of Mediterranean cookery, culinary imagination and highest sophistication. Excellent wine list and cheeseboard. *Menu from 73 euros | closed Sun, Mon and Aug | Beltrán i Rózpide, 16 | tel. 9 32 03 84 08 | www.neichel.es | Metro: María Cristina (L3)*

Via Veneto (127 F3) (*Ⓜ G 6*)
For more than 30 years this luxurious restaurant with classic décor has been a site of pilgrimage for hardcore gourmets, constantly developing and perfecting haute cuisine anchored in Catalan tradition. *Menu from 90 euros | closed Sat lunchtime and Sun | Ganduxer, 10 | tel. 9 32 00 72 44 | www.via venetorestaurant.com | bus: Av. Diagonal – Av. Sarrià (6, 7, 33, 34, 67, 68)*

Casa Leopoldo: traditional Catalan fare, served in a cosy ambience

oil and toasted breadcrumbs. Elegantly styled interior. Menus only. *Closed Sat lunchtime and Sun | Industria, 79 | tel. 9 32 07 61 15 | Metro: Verdaguer (L4, L5)*

BOTAFUMEIRO
(128 C4) (*ᗯ J 6*)

Traditional Galician cuisine – a culinary paradise for all lovers of fish and crustaceans. The tasting portions served at the counter are excellent too. *Daily | Gran de Gràcia, 81 | tel. 9 32 18 42 30 | Metro: Fontana (L3)*

CASA LEOPOLDO
(122 B4) (*ᗯ H 10*)

This Old Town restaurant has been a legend since the 1929 World Exhibition. The atmosphere is cosy and rustic, the food traditionally Catalan. *Closed Sun evening and Mon | Sant Rafael, 24 | tel. 9 34 41 30 14 | Metro: Parallel (L3)*

COMERÇ 24
(123 F4) (*ᗯ K 10*)

For lovers of fine avant-garde food: for many years, master chef Carles Abellán worked with the legendary Ferran Adrià, as evident from his sophisticated tapas! Michelin star. *Closed Sun and Mon | Comerç, 24 | tel. 9 33 19 21 02 | Metro: Jaume I (L4)*

GRESCA
(128 B6) (*ᗯ H 7*)

Young chef Rafael Peña, one of the gastronomic discoveries of the past few years, is enriching Catalan cuisine with surprising ideas such as octopus carpaccio with black pudding – original creations infused with the tastes of the chef's culinary perambulations abroad. The small restaurant has simple furnishings and a friendly attitude. Recommended lunch menu. *Closed Sat lunchtime and Sun | Provença, 230 | tel. 9 34 51 61 93 | Metro: Diagonal (L3, L5)*

HOFMANN ★ (128 B4) (*m H 6*)

Many famous chefs de cuisine have emerged from May Hofmann's school of high cuisine. The Michelin-starred food tastes of imagination and sophistication. *Closed Sat, Sun, public holidays and in*

9 34 92 92 92 | Metro: Passeig de Gràcia (L2, L3, L4)

MOO (128 C5) (*m J 7*)

Experience the exquisite Mediterranean cookery of the Roca brothers, garlanded

Hofmann: where the high art of fine cuisine reigns supreme

Aug | La Granada del Penedés, 14–16 | tel. 9 32 18 71 65 | Metro: Diagonal (L3, L5)

INSIDER TIP LOIDI
(128 C6) (*m J 8*)

Haute cuisine in a bistro under the auspices of Martín Berasategui. Allow Spanish star chef's original creations to melt in your mouth in the Catalan branch of his gastronomic empire (boasting by now six Michelin stars), without unduly stretching your budget. Changing four-course daily menus 40–60 euros. *Closed Sun evening | Mallorca, 248 | Hotel Condes de Barcelona | tel.*

with two Michelin stars and managers of one of the best Spanish restaurants in Girona. Ultra-chic design with a touch of Zen. *Closed Sun | Rosseló, 265 | in the lobby of the Omm hotel | tel. 9 34 45 40 00 | Metro: Diagonal (L3, L5)*

SAÜC (123 E2) (*m J 9*)

Award-winning young chef Xavier Franco enjoys experimenting with traditional Catalan recipes. Despite his avant-garde ambitions you can taste the essence of regional cuisine in dishes such as beef cheeks with apricots and thyme bacon. This small friendly restaurant has only eleven tables, but a Michelin star. *Closed Sun and Mon | Via Laietana, 49 | tel. 9 33 21 01 89 | Metro: Urquinaona (L1, L4)*

TRAGALUZ (128 C5) (*∅ J 7*)

Elegantly styled gourmet restaurant, a few steps away from Passeig de Gràcia, with an award-winning light-filled interior co-designed by star designer Mariscal. Fine modern cuisine from all around the Mediterranean. The ground floor houses an oyster bar, a sushi counter and a Japanese restaurant. *Daily | Passatge de la Concepció, 5 | tel. 9 34 87 01 96 | Metro: Diagonal (L3, L5)*

XIRINGUITO ESCRIBÀ
(136 B5) (*∅ N 11*)

This restaurant right on the beach, headed by Joan Escribà, is famous for his rice and pasta stir-fries, prepared right in front of guests' eyes. The daily menu includes fish and seafood straight off the boat. The delicious desserts are provided by Joan's father, city-wide famous pastry chef Antoni Escribà. *Closed Sun eve and Mon | Litoral Mar, 42 | Bogatell | tel. 9 32 21 07 29 | Metro: Llacuna (L4)*

RESTAURANTS: MODERATE

AGUA ☽ (135 E6) (*∅ L 11*)

Design restaurant with sea views. Fresh Mediterranean dishes. Pretty beach terrace. Booking essential! *Daily | Passeig Marítim de la Barceloneta, 30 | tel. 9 32 25 12 72 | Metro: Ciutadella (L4)*

ALLIUM (122 C4) (*∅ J 10*) ☺

This restaurant with light furnishings in the heart of the Gothic quarter serves Catalan cuisine following Slow Food rules: produce sourced locally, from ecological and organic agriculture or sustainable fisheries. Kitchen open right through the day until 11.30pm. *Daily | Call, 17 | tel. 9 33 02 30 03 | Metro: Jaume I (L4)*

BESTIAL ☽ (135 E5) (*∅ L 11*)

Its large and pretty terrace with sea views makes this beach bistro a hot tip for summer nights. Italian cuisine. *Daily | Ramón Trias Fargas, 2–4 | tel. 9 32 24 04 07 | Metro: Ciutadella (L4)*

CAL PEP ★ (123 E5) (*∅ J 10*)

Fish and seafood from the counter of this usually very full restaurant. Everything is prepared fresh in front of your eyes. Book ahead for the cosy restaurant in the back room! *Closed Mon lunchtime and Sun | Plaça de les Olles, 49 | tel. 9 33 10 79 61 | Metro: Barceloneta (L4)*

LOW BUDGET

▶ Narrow, crammed, noisy, hip – and unbeatable prices: the modern Old Town eatery *Can Nabo* (daily | **(134 B4)** (*∅ H 11*) Nou de Sant Francesc, 25 | Metro: Drassanes (L3) serves up a daily filling and tasty all-day menu from 4.50 euros, incl. a vegetarian option. On the menu are salads, risottos, fresh pasta, homemade pizzas or cakes.

▶ Not pretty, but incredibly good value: near the Rambla, Romesco (closed Sun | **(134 B4)** (*∅ H 10*) Sant Pau, 28 | tel. 9 33 18 93 81 | Metro: Liceu (L3) offers hearty fare: chicken with a side (3.90 euros), hake or cutlets (4.90 euros) and soups (2.60 euros).

INSIDER TIP ▶ CUINES DE SANTA CATERINA (123 E3) (*∅ J 10*)

At the stalls of this innovatively renovated market hall you can have breakfast, and gorge yourself on Mediterranean, Asian or vegetarian tapas. Everything fresh from the market. *Daily | Mercat de Santa Caterina | Av. Francesc Cambó, 16 | tel. 9 32 68 99 18 | Metro: Jaume I (L4)*

EN VILLE (122 B3) (*∅ J 10*)

Mirrors, marble tables and 1920s décor in the style of a French bistro. Good food, Mediterranean and market-fresh. Always jam-packed around lunchtime, thanks to the popular lunch menu! *Closed Sun | Doctor Dou, 14 | tel. 9 33 02 84 67 | Metro: Catalunya (L1, L3)*

HÁBALUC (128 B6) (*∅ H 7*) ☺

Eat healthily and enjoy tasty and imaginatively prepared vegetarian dishes and ecological produce. Street terrace. *Closed Sun | Enric Granados, 41 | tel. 9 34 52 29 28 | Metro: Diagonal (L3, L5)*

LA FONTAINE (133 E3) (*∅ F 10*)

Artists in particular enjoy this bar restaurant in Poble Sec. Mediterranean-Asian cuisine, friendly service, relaxed atmosphere. Homemade cheesecake, and the menu includes vegetarian and gluten-free dishes too. *Daily | França Xica, 20 | tel. 9 34 43 35 23 | Metro: Poble Sec (L3)*

INSIDER TIP ▶ LA VENTA ✲ (125 F3) (*∅ J 2*)

Enjoy even winter views from Tibidabo on the heated terraces of this pretty garden restaurant, while tucking into Mediterranean dishes. Booking recommended! *Closed Sun | Plaça Doctor Andreu | tel. 9 32 12 64 55 | Metro: Tibidabo, last stop of Tramvía Blau or bus no. 196 (to 10pm)*

Pinotxo in the Boqueria market hall: a simple counter, but haute cuisine

MERCAT DE LA BOQUERIA ⭐ (122 C3) (⌀ H 10)

Locals too enjoy eating at the Boqueria market. The *Pinotxo* counter *(stall 466–470)* of city-wide fame attracts even top chefs *(closed Sun)* after their market shop. A culinary institution with a price tag to match. Try the daily menu at the counter of *Kiosko Universal (stall 691)*, always crowded at lunchtime *(closed Sun)* or *El Quim de la Boqeria (stall 584)* for more authentic gourmet fare *(closed Sun and Mon)*. Metro: Liceu (L3)

SANTA MARIA (123 F4) (⌀ K 10)

Modern tapas restaurant: creative cuisine presented simply, at realistic prices. The ambience is cosmopolitan and relaxed. *Closed Sun and Mon | Commerç, 17 | tel. 9 33 15 12 27 | Metro: Jaume I (L4)*

SENYOR PARELLADA (123 E5) (⌀ J 10)

Popular restaurant in a medieval town palace, a modern version of a traditional Catalan tavern. Relaxed ambience, market-fresh food. *Daily | Argentaria, 37 | tel. 9 33 10 50 94 | Metro: Jaume I (L4)*

SET PORTES (123 E5) (⌀ J 11)

A gastronomic institution, serving traditional Catalan food in cosy Old Town atmosphere, only a few steps from the port. *Daily | Passeig Isabel II, 14 | tel. 9 33 19 30 33 | Metro: Barceloneta (L4)*

SILENUS (122 B3) (⌀ H 9)

Modern restaurant with creative décor, offering culinary culture from all around the Mediterranean. *Closed Sun | Carrer dels Àngels, 8 | tel. 9 33 02 26 80 | Metro: Catalunya (L1, L3)*

INSIDER TIP ▶ SURENY (129 D4) (⌀ J 6)

The high art of modern tapas, served in rustic, cosy ambience. Book a table if planning to visit on Friday or Saturday! Evenings only, closed Mon | Plaça Revolución, 17 | tel. 9 32 13 75 56 | Metro: Fontana (L3) or Joanic (L4)

RESTAURANTS: BUDGET

ÁNIMA (122 B3) (⌀ H 9)

Modern and originally furnished eatery, serving cosmopolitan dishes prepared right in front of guests' eyes. Lunchtime menus too. *Closed Sun | Àngels, 6 | tel. 9 33 42 49 12 | Metro: Catalunya (L1, L3)*

CAN CULLERETES (124 C4) (⌀ H 10)

The oldest restaurant in town was a regular haunt of literary folk and artists, of whom photos and paintings hang in the dining rooms. The menu features mainly traditional Catalan dishes. *Closed Sun eve and Mon | Quintana, 5 | tel. 9 33 17 64 85 | Metro: Liceu (L3)*

CAN MAÑO (135 D5) (⌀ K 11)

This restaurant in Barceloneta looks like the set for an Italian film from the 1960s. Fish fresh off the boat, prepared simply and with love. Book a table in good time, if you want to beat the locals to it. *Closed Sat eve, Sun and Mon lunchtime | Baluard, 12 | tel. 9 33 19 30 82 | Metro: Barceloneta (L4)*

ILLA DE GRÀCIA (128 C4) (⌀ J 6) ☺

Decoratively unrendered stone walls, light and minimalist furnishings: this restaurant in Gràcia is proof that when Barcelona's organic bohemians want to eat healthily, they see no reason to forego pleasure and trendy surroundings. Dishes are good and inexpensive, with some of the ingredients from organic agriculture. Good-value lunchtime menu on weekdays. *Closed Mon | Sant Domènec, 19 | tel. 9 32 38 02 29 | Metro: Fontana (L3)*

LOCAL SPECIALITIES

▶ **Allioli** – fine olive oil mayonnaise with garlic, served with fish or rice dishes or grilled meat (photo left)

▶ **Amanida catalana** – salad with embotits, smoked sausage products

▶ **Arròs negre** – rice with squid including the ink, which lends the dish its black colour and special aroma

▶ **Bacallà** – cod is prepared following various recipes: a la samfaina for instance (with tomatoes, paprika, aubergines), chilli and garlic (al pil-pil) or honey

▶ **Canelones a la catalana** – cannelloni Catalan-style, filled with mincemeat, chicken breast and liver, topped and baked with béchamel sauce

▶ **Cava** – Catalan sparkling wine, traditionally matured in bottles; the best don't have to fear the taste test with champagne

▶ **Crema catalana** – sweet egg custard, covered with a layer of caramelised sugar

▶ **Escalivada** – cold starter of grilled peppers and aubergines in olive oil

▶ **Espinacs a la catalana** – Starter of spinach (or chard) with raisins and pine kernels

▶ **Esqueixada** – popular starter made from raw cod, fresh tomatoes, onions, peppers and black olives

▶ **Fideuà** – pasta paella with monkfish, squid, prawns, mussels, baked in the oven

▶ **Llagosta i pollastre** – chicken with langouste, in tomato-hazelnut sauce or with almonds, chocolate, saffron and garlic

▶ **Pa amb tomàquet** – bread, rubbed with garlic and tomato and drizzled with olive oil. For the Catalans, this starter is national dish, philosophy and passion

▶ **Suquet de peix** – Catalan fish soup, usually a mix of monkfish, sea bream, squid and seafood (photo right)

LA AVIA (134 A3) (*Ø G 10*)
Design boom and nouvelle cuisine have left no trace at this familiar Raval eatery with bohemian style. The menu features traditional Catalan dishes such as bean stew, paella or squid à la marinera with potatoes and peas at dumping prices from 3.60 euros. Tasty homemade giant empanadas 1.20 euros. *Daily | La Cera, 33 | tel. 9 34 42 00 97 | Metro: Sant Antoni (L2)*

LA BELLA NAPOLI (133 F3) (*G 10*)

Excellent stone-oven pizzas, as authentically Italian as the ambience, service and atmosphere. This is a popular restaurant, so book or go early in the evening. *Closed Tue lunchtime and Mon | Margarit, 14 | tel. 9 34 42 50 56 | Metro: Poble Sec (L3)*

LA BOMBETA (135 D5) (*J 11*)

Here at this rustic eatery in the fishing village of Barceloneta the *bombetas,* little bombs, that gave the place its name, are still made at home: fried balls of mashed potato with a meat filling, hot sauce and aioli. The grilled hake or calamari. are also very tasty No credit cards. *Closed Wed | Maquinista, 3 | tel. 9 33 19 94 45 | Metro: Barceloneta (L4)*

INSIDER TIP LA CANDELA
(123 F3) (*K 9*)

Market-fresh, imaginative cuisine at realistic prices on one of the Old Town's most beautiful terraces, on a charming square with historic ambience. *Closed Sun | Plaça de Sant Pere, 12 | tel. 9 33 10 62 42 | Metro: Arc de Triomf (L1)*

LA CERERÍA (134 B4) (*J 10*)

Vegetarian fare in a cosy Old Town atmosphere. Homemade cake, pizza and antipasti, mostly from organic agriculture. *Closed Sun | Baixada de Sant Miquel, 3 | tel. 9 33 01 85 10 | Metro: Liceu (L3)*

ORGANIC (122 B4) (*H 10*)

All produce stems from organic agriculture. Relaxed atmosphere, young clientele, a few paces from the Rambla. *Daily | Junta de Commerç, 11 | tel. 9 33 01 09 02 | Metro: Liceu (L1, L3)*

PLA DELS ÀNGELS (122 B2) (*H 9*)

Modern, originally designed eatery opposite the Museum of Contemporary

For those with a sweet tooth: crema catalana

Art. Fresh Mediterranean dishes, lunchtime menus. *Daily | Ferlandina, 23 | tel. 9 33 29 40 47 | Metro: Universitat (L1, L2)*

SÉSAMO (122 A3) (*G 9*)

Cosy vegetarian restaurant serving breakfast, a lunch menu and imaginative dishes in the evening. *Closed Tue | Sant Antoni Abat, 52 | tel. 9 34 41 64 11 | Metro: Sant Antoni (L2)*

SHOPPING

CITY WHERE TO START?

Barcelona doesn't have that one famous shopping street as other cities do. Exclusive boutiques can be found mainly along the Rambla de Catalunya **(128 B5–6; 134 B1)** *(⚲ J 7–8)* (above Plaça de Catalunya!) and Passeig de Gràcia **(128 C5–6; 134 C1–2)** *(⚲ J 8–9)*. Trendy shops and fashion chain stores have set up at Porta de l'Àngel **(123 D2–3)** *(⚲ J 9)* and in the Portaferrissa alley **(122 C3)** *(⚲ H–J 10)*, while Carrer Girona **(123 F1–2)** *(⚲ K 9)* has become an inner-city outlet street.

'I shop, therefore I am': it's no coincidence that a famous design department store in Barcelona chose this ironically adapted aphorism as its advertising slogan.

The Catalans have always been keen on making their identity shine in the most impressive way – as illustrated by many exclusive shops, especially in the upper part of the city, whether in splendid Art Nouveau or upmarket post-modern understatement. In the Old Town you'll also find small corner shops, long-established general stores, kitsch, crafts or junk – often in tiny spaces where time seems to have stood still.

Recently more and more trendy shops and hip fashion boutiques have opened

Photo: Shop window in the Old Town

From a junkshop to the latest thing: fashion temples and trendy shops, Mediterranean markets and antiquarians

up in Raval, around Carrer Avinyó or in the Santa Caterina quarter. In the Ribera quarter delightful shops for crafts, designer clothes and delicatessen cluster around Passeig del Born and the Rec alleyway. But note: many shops in the Ribera quarter stay closed on a Monday! If you prefer multicultural or little alternative shops and organic boheme, head for the Gràcia quarter.

While shopping in Barcelona is great fun, it's not exactly cheap. According to

statistics, prices here are above those of London or New York. Forget fans and flamenco dancers – here you are in a European bastion of design, fashion and crafts. Look out when purchasing crafts, so you don't end up with 'typical Catalan' goods made in Hong Kong. The information points of the tourist office have a list of recommended shops. Barcelona's museum shops are a good source for gift ideas.

Usual opening hours are Monday to

ANTIQUES

Friday between 10am and 2.30pm and again from 4.30 to 8pm. The major shopping centres and department stores are usually open till 10pm, often Saturday too.

ANTIQUES

Barcelona is a mecca for (solvent) lovers of Catalan Art Nouveau. A tip for less

Call. The most interesting shops here are in the Carrer de la Palla and in the Carrer dels Banys Nous alley.

BOOKS & MUSIC

If you're looking for art books, coffee-table books or exhibition catalogues: the museum bookshops stock offer an excellent selection, especially in those

Chocolaterie Fargas: sweet treats behind an Art Nouveau façade

well-endowed travellers: take a look at the shops around the Encants Nous flea market; don't be put off by their occasional shabbiness.

OLD TOWN ★
(122–123 C–D 3–4) (*∅ J 10*)
You'll find atmospheric antique dealers for looking and browsing in the medieval alleys of the former Jewish quarter of El

of the Miró Foundation, the Picasso Museum or the Centre for Contemporary Culture.

LA CENTRAL DEL RAVAL
(122 C2) (*∅ H 9*)
This Baroque chapel shelters one of the largest and best-stocked bookshops in Europe. *Elisabets, 6 | www.lacentral.com | Metro: Catalunya (L1, L3)*

DISCOS CASTELLÓ (134 B2) (*Ⓜ H 9*)
This long-established record shop is a must for music fans: whether new releases, cult or rarities – you'll be well looked-after. Second-hand vinyl and CDs from 3 euros. *Tallers, 7 | www.castello discos.com | Metro: Plaça Catalunya (L1, L3)*

DELICATESSEN, SPECIALITIES & MARKETS

CACAO SAMPAKA (134 B1) (*Ⓜ J 8*)
Pure cocoa culture, without additives: chocolate in surprising creations and aromas. *Café Mon–Sat 9am–8.30pm | Consell de Cent, 292 | www.cacaosampaka. com | Metro: Passeig de Gràcia (L2, L3, L4)*

INSIDER TIP **CAELUM** ●
(123 D3–4) (*Ⓜ J 10*)
Divine delicacies, made in Spanish monasteries and convents: pastries, marzipan, honey, wine, liqueurs. Try teas and Mass wines by candlelight and early music in the restored 14th-century cellar. *Shop Mon–Thu 10.30am–8.30pm, Fri and Sat* 11am–11.30pm, Sun 11.30am–8.30pm, cellar vaults Tue–Thu 3.30–8.30pm, Fri and Sat 3.30–11pm | www.caelum barcelona.com | Carrer de la Palla, 8 | Metro: Liceu (L3)

CASA GISBERT ★ (123 E5) (*Ⓜ J 10*)
Enchanting general store, over 150 years old, in the Ribera quarter. The oven where prunes and apricots are dried has been functioning since 1851 and is unique in all of Spain. *Closed Sun and Mon | Sombrerers, 23 | www.cangisbert. com | Metro: Jaume I (L4)*

FARGAS ★ (123 D3) (*Ⓜ J 10*)
Nobody, but nobody can resist the freshly prepared chocolate. The decor too is of excellent taste: this pretty Art Nouveau shop opened in 1827, when it was the first *xocolateria* in town. *Carrer del Pi, 16 | Metro: Catalunya (L1, L3)*

HERBOLARI DEL REI (122 C4) (*Ⓜ H 10*)
Well worth a visit, this shop opened in 1818 selling spices and Mediterranean herbs. *Vidre, 1 | Metro: Liceu (L3)*

★ **Old Town**
Browse in Barcelona's most interesting antique shops → p. 72

★ **Casa Gisbert**
Traditional general store like in great-grandmother's time → p. 73

★ **Fargas**
Sweet temptation → p. 73

★ **Mercat de Sant Josep/ La Boqueria**
Sensual shopping experience between modernisme and seafood → p. 74

★ **Vinçon**
Encounter a design department store of the third kind → p. 75

★ **Art Escudellers**
Catalan crafts: from tiles to ceramics → p. 75

★ **La Manual Alpargatera**
Made-to-measure shoes: walk on traditional soles → p. 77

★ **Textile route**
Modern designs within medieval walls → p. 75

MARCO POLO HIGHLIGHTS

INSIDER TIP ▶ LA PINEDA
(123 D3) (𝔐 J 10)

Tapas, sausage, wine: Catalan delicatessen products are for sale in this charming old general store where you can try the goods at the tasting tables. *Mon–Sat 9am–3pm and 6–9.30pm, Sun 11am–3pm | Pi, 16 | Metro: Liceu (L3)*

MERCAT DE SANT JOSEP/ LA BOQUERIA ★ ●
(122 C3) (𝔐 H 10)

The nickname for the famous market hall on La Rambla, La Boqueria, is the 'Belly of Barcelona'. Here, not only Catalan housewives but also the city's star chefs come here to buy. Admire the piled-up fresh fish and seafood, the mouth-watering mounds of mushrooms, chillies, nuts and truffles. Avoid the overpriced stalls at the entrance. And try the delicacies made from fresh produce at the stalls along the perimeter of the hall. *Closed Sun | Rambla, 85 | Metro: Liceu (L3)*

PASTELERÍA ESCRIBÀ ●
(122 C4) (𝔐 H 10)

A historic Art Nouveau patisserie with a richly ornate façade, one of the best places in Barcelona for those who love chocolate and all things sweet. *Rambla, 83 | www.escriba.es | Metro: Liceu (L3)*

QUEVIURES MURRIA
(128 C6) (𝔐 J 8)

This beautiful Art Nouveau-style general store, founded in 1898, sells fine foods such as cheese, ham, caviar, oils and chocolate. Home-produced *cava. Roger de Llùria, 85 | www.murria.cat | Metro: Passeig de Gràcia (L2, L3, L4)*

VILA VINITECA (123 E5) (𝔐 J 10)

Alongside top wines from the Priorat or cult vintages such as Vega Sicilia, there are 4000 other wines. Plus a rich selection of sherry, vermouth and rarities. *Agullers, 7 | Metro: Jaume I (L4)*

If you like design, your eyes will light up in the furniture department at Vinçon

DESIGN & CRAFTS

ALMACÉN MARABI (123 E4) (*⊞ J 10*)
This original workshop sells crafts made from fabric, brooches or key rings. *Flassaders, 30 | Metro: Jaume I (L4)*

ART ESCUDELLERS ⭐
(122 C5) (*⊞ H 10*)
Come here to find authentic crafts, whether traditional or contemporary, for realistic prices. Alongside beautiful tiles, there are ceramics and glass pieces, as well as original jewellery. *Escudellers, 12 and Escudellers, 23–25 (opposite) | www.escudellers-art.com | Metro: Drassanes (L3)*

INSIDER TIP ▶ CERERÍA SUBIRÁ
(123 D4) (*⊞ J 10*)
Lovely candle store where time seems to have stood still since 1761. *Closed Sat afternoon | Baixada de la Llibreteria, 7 | Metro: Jaume I (L4)*

D BARCELONA (128 C5) (*⊞ J 7*)
A good place for accessories and decorative items, fun presents and out-of-the-ordinary objects. *Diagonal, 367 | Metro: Diagonal (L3, L5)*

DOS I UNA (128 C5) (*⊞ J 7*)
Creative gifts, curiosities and kitsch from Catalunya. *Rosselló, 275 | Metro: Diagonal (L3, L5)*

TEXTILE ROUTE ⭐
(123 E4–5) (*⊞ J 10*)
For a long time the historic workmen's houses and weaver's workshops of the Ribera quarter stood empty. In the past years the buildings have been taken over and revived by young designers. Especially around the streets of Banys Vells, Esquirol Flassaders and Barra de Ferro, you'll find very interesting shops, textile workshops and trendy fashion studios. For sustenance, there are plenty of atmospheric cafés and bars. Just one thing: most shops are closed on Mondays. *Metro: Jaume I (L4)*

VINÇON ⭐ (128 C5) (*⊞ J 7*)
This was once one of the pioneering design shops in town, and it is still worth a visit. Also worth seeing is the furniture department: these rooms were once inhabited by the Art Nouveau painter Santiago Rusiñol. *Passeig de Gràcia, 96 | www.vincon.com | Metro: Diagonal (L3, L5)*

GALLERIES

Established galleries cluster in the streets of Consell de Cent/Rambla de Catalunya (134 B1) (*⊞ H–J 8*): e.g. *Carles Taché (Consell de Cent, 290)* or *Prats (Rambla de Catalunya, 54)*, representing important Spanish and Catalan artists. New galleries have sprung up in Raval, around the Museum of Contemporary Art and in Gràcia, in most recent times also in the Poble Nou quarter or around Santa Caterina market.

FASHION & ACCESSORIES

CUSTO (134 C4) (*J 10*)

In-your-face prints and material mix: the innovative tops und t-shirts by Custo are now available in more than 50 countries, and it all started in the late 1990s in this shop in the Old Town. *Plaça de les Olles, 7 | www.custo-barcelona.com | Metro: Jaume I (L4)*

DESIGUAL (134 C1) (*J 8*)

Garish patchwork clothing for ladies, gentlemen and children – with the craziest combinations of fabric and colours! You can save up to 50 per cent at this outlet – nobody will notice if you are wearing last year's model, as the popular Spanish label has remained true to its out-there style for over 25 years. *Diputación, 323 | www.desigual.com | Metro: Passeig de Gràcia (L2, L3) or Girona (L4)*

EL MERCADILLO
(123 D3) (*J 10*)

A super-trendy fashion bazaar for young people extending over several storeys. A crazy hair-dresser and a café with a lovely patio are part of the operation. *Portaferrissa, 1 | Metro: Liceu (L3)*

GUANTERÍA PEDRO ALONSO
(123 D3) (*J 9*)

In this Art Nouveau shop you'll find gloves for nearly every occasion, as well as fans. *Santa Anna, 27 | Metro: Catalunya (L1, L3)*

LA CUBANA (122 C4) (*H 10*)

Old-fashioned in the best sense of the world: selling lace, gloves and silk scarves, as well as hand-painted fans *(mantillas)* – this place has been a local legend since 1824. *Boqueria, 26 | Metro: Liceu (L3)*

RIERA BAIXA (122 B3) (*H 10*)

This small street, which at first glance might appear a bit shabby, is extremely hip: there are many second-hand shops, tattoo and piercing parlours as well as shops for vintage clothing. *Riera Baixa | Metro: Liceu (L3)*

SOMBRERERÍA OBACH
(123 D4) (*J 10*)

Traditional hattery in a picturesque corner shop. The lore of which hat fits which kind of head has been passed on here for generations. *Call, 2 | Metro: Liceu (L3)*

or Miss Sixty. You can save up to half on the retail price in the outlet near the Met-

No-go zone for purists: at Desigual wild combinations of crazy colours are the order of the day

SHOES

CAMPER

While the eminently wearable shoes are now famous the world over, they are still a lot cheaper in Spain than elsewhere. *El Triangle | (123 D2) (ØJ J 9) Plaça Catalunya | Metro: Catalunya (L1, L3) | (128 C6) (ØJ J 8) València, 249 | Metro: Passeig de Gràcia (L2, L3, L4)*

CASAS (128 C3) (ØJ J 5)

Whether sporty, classically chic or ultra-modern – this Catalan company has the fitting shoe for nearly every foot, from their own models to brands such as Vialis, Café Noir, Camper, Moschino, Marc Jacob

ro station Lesseps – shoe fans on their way to Parc Güell simply get off one station earlier. *Outlet Mon–Sat 10am–2pm and 5–8.30pm | Gran de Gràcia, 239 | for a list of branches see www.ucasas.com | Metro: Lesseps (L3)*

LA MANUAL ALPARGATERA ★ (123 D5) (ØJ J 10)

The popular *espardenyes,* linen shoes on raffia soles, have been made to measure in this down-to-earth family concern for many generations: whether for drop-in customers or for VIP feet such as those of Hollywood actor Michael Douglas. *Avinyó, 7 | Metro: Liceu (L3)*

ENTERTAINMENT

CITY **WHERE TO START?**
There is no particular nightlife neighbourhood – the night owls spread out. In the **Old Town** you'll meet the cool city bohemians and young people. In **Raval** a new café and bar scene has sprung up, the outlandish avant-garde rubbing shoulders with cosy taverns. Enormously in is the **Ribera quarter**, with cocktail bars, trendy eateries and industrial lofts converted into hip bars, especially around the Passeig del Born and Mercat del Born. Some of the coolest clubs and lounges are by the beach between Barceloneta and Vila Olímpica.

Whether your tastes run to elegant or rustic, eccentric or cosy, vintage, chintzy or post-modern: Barcelona's night life offers something for everybody.

The Santa Caterina neighbourhood is seeing the birth of a new scene with trendy places to meet and chillout bars, especially around the market hall and the atmospheric **INSIDER TIP** Plaça D'Allada-Vermell. The Gràcia quarter has an alternative vibe, with countless small pubs, tapas bars and some very good-value restaurants. In summer many squares turn into busy café terraces and open-air stages for musicians, street artists or jugglers. Between the long-established bars and small cafés in Poble Sec a number of cult bars have set up shop off the beaten tourist track – particularly

Photo: Salsa club

The perfect place for night owls: taverns and dance palaces, techno clubs and concert halls – take your pick!

around the streets Blai and Blesa. The Zona Alta (Upper Town) around Diagonal, Mariano Cubí and Tibidabo is the stomping ground of the fashion and career-conscious. Some design bars in Eixample are now a bit passé. In summer, many hotels open their ☀️ INSIDERTIP roof terraces as bars and lounges. The terraces of the fancy *Casa Fuster* hotel, the *Majestic* or *H 1898* are particularly beautiful. From the terraces of the hip *W Hotel* or the elegant *Arts Barcelona* hotel – closer to the ground, but still very nice – you have a fantastic view of the sea. One word of warning: be on your guard in the Old Town: leave your valuables at home and take a taxi!

BARS & LOUNGES

BOADAS ⭐ (122 C2) (*Ⓜ H 9*)
This legendary cocktail bar is the oldest in Barcelona and still a legend; Ernest Hemingway, no less, drank his mojito here. *Mon–Sat 12 noon–2am | Tallers, 1 | Metro: Catalunya (L1, L3)*

Blue Hour in Barcelona with a drink on the Plaça de Santa Maria del Mar

INSIDER TIP CABART (133 F4) (*Ⓜ G 11*)
Hairdressers' drying hoods turned into lamps and traffic lights on the wall are not the only curiosities in this cult Poble Sec bar. Or do you normally drink your beer sitting in a bath tub? *Closed Sun and Mon | Piquer, 27 | Metro: Parallel (L3)*

CANIGÓ (129 D4) (*Ⓜ K 6*)
For those who have seen enough super-styled lounges in Barcelona and would like to know what a Catalan pub looks like, this is the right place. In the evenings, this traditional bar in the Gràcia neighbourhood is often jam-packed and noisy, even without piped music. *Thu 5pm–2.30am, Fri 5pm–3am, Sat 8pm–3am | Verdi, 2 | Metro: Fontana (L3))*

CASA ALMIRALL (122 B2) (*Ⓜ H 9*)
Marble counter, modernist lamps and Art Nouveau décor: a classic Barcelona bar that has been around since 1860. The retro bar is very popular with young people too. *Daily from 7pm | Joaquín Costa, 33 | Metro: Universitat (L1, L2)*

CDLC (CARPE DIEM LOUNGE CLUB) ●
(135 E5) (*Ⓜ L 11*)
The cool beach terrace with a view of the Mediterranean offers relaxing Balinese loungers. Inside, a huge club with VIP lounges, dance floors and DJ sessions. *Daily 12 noon–2am | Passeig Marítim, 32 | tel. 9 32 24 04 70 | Metro: Ciutadella (L4)*

CHATELET (129 D4) (*Ⓜ K 6*)
This could be the living room of a cutting-edge designer and flea market freak: one of the most popular bars in Gràcia. Cocktails ordered before 10pm only cost 4 euros. *Daily 6pm–2.30am | Torrijos 54 | Metro: Fontana (L3)*

DRY MARTINI (128 B5) (𝄢 H 7)
Named after the favourite drink of Spanish director Luis Buñuel: a must for cocktail fans. Delicious little snacks are served with the drinks. *Daily from 6.30pm | Aribau, 162 | Metro: Hospital Clínic (L5)*

GIMLET (123 E4) (𝄢 K 10)
A classic choice for bohemians with a bit of money and nonconformist night owls with a penchant for a proper drink. *Mon–Sat from 8pm | Rec, 24 | Metro: Jaume I (L4)*

LONDON BAR (122 B5) (𝄢 H 10)
If the thick cigarette fug should lift, you'll be able to make out the crumbling charm of a bohemian bar that has been popular since 1910. *Tue–Sun from 7pm | Nou de la Rambla, 34 | Metro: Liceu (L3)*

LUPARA (134 C3) (𝄢 J 10)
Small but perfectly formed trendy bar with terrace in the new entertainment district around the Santa Caterina market hall. This is where Barcelona's bohemians enjoy a well-poured drink with tasty sausage and cheese tapas. *Sun–Thu 12 noon–12 midnight, Fri and Sat 12 noon–3am | Plaça de Santa Caterina, 2 | Metro: Jaume I (L4)*

MARGARITA BLUE (122 C6) (𝄢 H 11)
Curious pub and Tex-Mex restaurant, often packed to the doors. DJs, drinks and cocktails. *Daily from 7pm | Josep Anselm Clavé, 6 | Metro: Drassanes (L3)*

MIRABÉ ☀ (125 F3) (𝄢 J 2)
Aperitifs and long drinks – and a INSIDERTIP breathtaking view across the whole of Barcelona. In the summer there's a garden terrace. *Tue–Sun 7pm–2am | Manuel Arnús, 2 | FGC: Tibidabo, change to Tramvía Blau or bus no. 196*

INSIDERTIP ▶ PIPA CLUB
(122 C4–5) (𝄢 H 10)
This original cosy trendy bar with views of Plaça Reial is located in the pipe smokers' private club. Don't forget you have to ring the doorbell of the house! *Daily 11pm–1.30am | Plaça Reial, 3, pral. | Metro: Liceu (L3)*

PITÍN BAR (123 E5) (𝄢 K 10)
Small, intimate and originally designed bar at the heart of the Ribera neighbourhood. Popular terrace. *Tue–Fri from 10am, Sat, Sun from 11am | Pg. Del Born, 34 | Metro: Jaume I (L4)*

RESOLIS (134 A3) (𝄢 H 10)
This long-established bar in Raval is one of the few trendy bars that still show their modernisme origins. Basic, rustic and easy-going. Delicious snacks prepare the stomach for a longer tour on the tiles. *Sun–Fri 5pm–midnight, Sat 5pm–2am |*

★ **Boadas**
In Hemingway's footsteps: Barcelona's legendary cocktail bar
→ p. 79

★ **Jamboree**
Best jazz cellar in town → p. 83

★ **Sala Apolo/Nitsa Club**
Trendy club in a former ballroom → p. 83

★ **Gran Teatre del Liceu**
More than just an opera house: a symbol of Catalan culture → p. 84

★ **Palau de la Música Catalana**
Splendid concert hall in Art Nouveau style → p. 85

MARCO POLO HIGHLIGHTS

Carrer Riera Baixa, 22 | Metro: Sant Antoni (L2)

SÓ-LÓ BAR (133 F3) ( *G 10*)

No trace of the current drinks brands, screens or other trendy staples: instead the most outlandish types of rum, with over 60 bottles occupying the shelf of this spacious trendy bar in Poble Sec. Up to 11pm all cocktails cost 4 euros. *Closed Sun | Margarit, 18 | Metro: Parallel (L3)*

SUBORN (123 F5) (*K 10*)

Relaxed hipster spot in a modern loft in the in-quarter of Born: the restaurant *(Tue–Sun 8pm–midnight)* serves Mediterranean dishes. With club, dance floor and terrace. *Thu–Sat from midnight | Ribera, 18 | tel. 9 33 10 11 10 | Metro: Barceloneta (L4)*

INSIDER TIP ▶ XIX (133 E2) (*F 9*)

Original cocktail bar, known for its excellent gin & tonic. More than 30 gin brands await you behind a marble counter that's over 100 years old. *Closed Sun | Rocafort, 19 | Metro: Poble Sec (L3)*

DISCOS, CLUBS & LIVE MUSIC

The action really only starts after midnight. Mostly at weekends, many clubs offer live music too, or live clubs will function as clubs outside performance times. Live performances start earlier, usually from 9 or 10pm.

ANTILLA BARCELONA (134 A1) (*G 8*)

One of the leading salsa clubs, where immigrants from the Caribbean dance their homesickness away. *Tue–Sun from 11pm | Aragó, 141 | www.antillasalsa.com | Metro: Hospital Clínic (L5)*

BIKINI (127 E3) (*F 6*)

From pop to electronic dance – this popular club will play it all. Salsa dance room, cocktail bar, concerts. *Wed–Sat from midnight | Déu i Mata, 105 | www.bikini bcn.com | Metro: Les Corts (L3)*

CITY HALL (122 C5) (*J 9*)

Electronic music and techno in a theatre backdrop from times past, put on by top DJs from Spain and abroad, and a pretty

You'll feel like you're at the movies: the trendy Opium club shows films too

terrace in the summer. One of the most popular clubs in the city centre. *Daily from midnight | Rambla de Catalunya, 4 | www.ottozutz.es | Metro: Plaça Catalunya (L1, L3)*

JAMBOREE ★ (122 C4–5) (*⊞ H 10*)

This jazz cellar has been a meeting point for connoisseurs since 1959. Performances by international guests, dance floor. *Daily live music 9 and 11pm, disco from 1am | Plaça Reial, 17 | www.masimas.com | Metro: Liceu (L3)*

INSIDERTIP JAZZ SI CLUB
(122 A2–3) (*⊞ G 9*)

Hidden in a Raval alley: popular bar with live performances by young musicians. Drinks at very reasonable prices. Jazz, flamenco, jam sessions. *Daily, varying opening times | Requesens, 2 | tel. 9 33 29 00 20 | www.tallerdemusics.com | Metro: Sant Antoni (L2)*

LUZ DE GAS (128 A4) (*⊞ H 6*)

Popular disco and music hall with wonderfully decadent Belle Époque kitsch. Interesting live programmes, espe-

cially during the jazz festival (Oct–Dec). *Daily from 11.30pm | Muntaner, 246 | tel. 9 32 09 73 85 | www.luzdegas.com | Metro: Diagonal (L3, L5)*

MARULA CAFÉ (122 C5) (*⊞ H 10*)

Black music, soul, funk, Latin jazz, disco, also for more mature clubbers. *Daily from 11pm | Escudellers, 49 | Metro: Drassanes (L3)*

MOOG (1220 B5) (*⊞ H 10*)

Excellent music programme with well-known DJs. For lovers of techno and house. *Daily from midnight | Arc del Teatre, 3 | www.masimas.com | Metro: Liceu (L3)*

OPIUM (128 B5) (*⊞ H 7*)

Exclusive club in a former cinema. Three spacious bars, a small dance floor, film showings. Very popular with the fashion-conscious crowd. *Tue–Sun from 11.30pm | Paris, 193–197 | Metro: Diagonal (L3, L5)*

OTTO ZUTZ CLUB (128 B3) (*⊞ H 6*)

This industrial-look club spanning three floors has been a hit for over 20 years. DJ sessions, electronic and Black music. Things only get going for real around 2am. *Wed–Sat from midnight | Lincoln, 15 | www.ottozutz.com | FGC: Gràcia, Metro: Fontana (L3)*

23 ROBADOR (122 B4) (*⊞ H 10*)

Graffiti on the stone walls, a whiff of underground. On Wednesdays there's jazz, on Sundays flamenco, at other times DJs spin their stuff. Ring the doorbell of the house to get in! *Closed Mon | Robador, 23 | Metro: Liceu (L3)*

SALA APOLO/NITSA CLUB ★
(122 A5) (*⊞ G 10*)

An elegant former ballroom, today one of the hippest places in town – with live music, disco, DJs, dance parties, underground films and every Wednesday evening the ● rumba night. At the weekend, Sala Apolo turns into the Nitsa Club, playing current musical trends in various rooms. *Sala Apolo daily, Nitsa Club Fri and Sat from 12.30am | Nou de la Rambla, 113 | www.sala-apolo.com | Metro: Parallel (L3)*

SHOKO ☸ (135 E6) (*∅ L 11*)

Lounge club and restaurant with sea view. One of the most sought-after beach terraces in town, playing 1980s music, funk and house. International DJs. *Daily from midnight | Passeig Marítim de*

LOW BUDGET

▶ This is how you'd imagine a cosy tavern in the port area: at *Can Paixano (Mon–Sat 9am–10.30pm |* **(134 C5)** *(∅ J 11) | Reina Cristina, 7 | www.canpaixano.com | Metro: Barceloneta (L4)*, hams hang from the ceiling beams and the walls are decoratively yellowed. Drinks are taken standing up, there are no chairs. House cava at rock-bottom prices of 0.80–1.20 euros per glass.

▶ You'll be glad to hear that there's a way to party away in the hippest clubs in town, such as the Shoko – for free! All you have to do is get onto the right guest list: one of the most popular is ● Shaz's guest list under *www.barcelonaparties.com*. Watch out though: the invites are only valid for that specific time – latecomers have to pay, up to 20 euros. So get in line in good time, as long queues will form.

la Barceloneta, 36 | Metro: Ciutadella (L4)

TABLAO DE CARMEN (132 C2) (*∅ E 9*)

Where the Tablao de Carmen stands today, the legendary flamenco dancer Carmen Amaya debuted for the opening of the World Exhibition in 1929. Authentic flamenco and a programme for the discerning. In the Poble Espanyol museum village. *Tue–Sun approx. 8pm–2am, flamenco shows Tue–Sun 7.45 and 10pm | 34 euros incl. drink and admission to Poble Espanyol | www.tablaodecarmen. com | Metro: Espanya (L1, L3), onwards on foot or by bus: Poble Espanyol (61, 13)*

TARANTOS (122 C4) (*∅ H 10*)

Many great names of flamenco have performed here, from Antonio Gades to Duquende. *Tue–Sat from 9.30pm, live flamenco at 9.30, 10.30pm, later disco and Musica Latina | admission flamenco bar 5 euros | Plaça Reial, 17 | Metro: Liceu (L3)*

CONCERT HALLS & OPERA

AUDITORI DE BARCELONA (AUDITORIUM) (135 F2) (*∅ L 9*)

Designed by Rafael Moneo and inaugurated in 1999, the building next to the national theatre is the modern heart of concert life. International top stars perform in the auditorium, and the symphony orchestra is also based here. *Lepant, 150 | tel. 932479300 | www. auditori.com | Metro: Monumental (L2), Glòries (L1)*

GRAN TEATRE DEL LICEU ★ (122 C4) (*∅ H 10*)

When the historic theatre on the Rambla burnt down in 1994, the flames not only destroyed one of Europe's most beautiful opera houses: the Liceu most of all symbolised the Catalans' self-confidence and culture, as a counterpoint to Madrid. While the auditorium has risen again in its old splendour, the stage is now amongst the world's most modern. Artistically too, this temple to the muses has been dusted down, with contemporary works and modern director's theatre alongside the traditional repertoire. *Rambla, 51–59 | tel. 9 34 85 99 13 | www. liceubarcelona.com | Metro: Liceu (L3)*

PALAU DE LA MÚSICA CATALANA ⭐
(123 E3) *(ℳ J 9)*
While all the Art Nouveau splendour in this concert hall makes it difficult to concentrate on the music, the programme merits undivided attention. Every year, over 200 concerts take place here, including international star performances – from classical via jazz to chanson or world music. *Sant Pere Més Alt | tel. 9 32 95 72 00 | www.palaumusica.org | Metro: Urquinaona (L1, L4)*

THEATRE

Barcelona has long since established itself internationally as a forum for new and discerning forms of theatre. Spain's most important independent ensembles are at home here: the Lliure theatre, troupes such as Els Joglars or La Fura dels Baus. Many theatres put on performances in the Catalan language. Most international performances can be caught at the Mercat de les Flors and during the *Grec* arts festival every July and August.

MERCAT DE LES FLORS
(133 D–E3) *(ℳ E 10)*
Contemporary theatre and dance of international calibre. In the former flower market guest performers from all over the world alternate with performances

Art Nouveau splendour in the Palau de la Música Catalana concert hall

by local artists. Also worth seeing is the dome above the entrance hall. Here, you'll see one of Miquel Barceló's most beautiful paintings. Around the Mercat a huge theatre complex has sprung up, including the renowned *Teatre Lliure (Teatre Fabià Puigserver)* in the imposing Palau de la Agricultura and the *Theatre Institute. Lleida, 59 | tel. 9 34 26 18 75 | Metro: Plaça Espanya (L1, L3)*

WHERE TO STAY

New top-level hotels keep springing up in Barcelona, particularly near the beach between the Olympic Village, Vila Olímpica, and the Forum.

Luxury and high-comfort hotels are opening up in stylishly renovated buildings in the Old Town, and trendy hotels are being inaugurated all over the city. Still, bed capacity is not sufficient when international conferences or trade fairs are taking place in Barcelona – and nearly every month has some big event.

At times like these hotels are not only booked long in advance, but also go for double and triple rates. And this on top of prices which by international comparison already occupy the top rank. On the other hand, at times with little demand you may get hold of highly attractive of-fers – rebates of up to 60 per cent or special discount packages. It's also always a good idea to book early, to avoid disappointment, as they say.

INSIDER TIP Do ask for a room giving onto the outside *(habitación exterior)* – a room giving onto the interior *(habitación interior)* with a window opening up to a light well, while nothing unusual in Barcelona, still has a somewhat depressing vibe (apart from nearly always being a lot smaller). If you're visiting in summer, book a room with air conditioning.

Also find out whether the price includes breakfast and value added tax (IVA)! The following information refers to the official price categories of the hotels. However, check the hotel's own websites to take advantage of the frequent special offers.

Photo: Hotel Palace

Sleep tight and in nice surroundings: book your hotel room early in Barcelona for a good night's rest

HOTELS: EXPENSIVE

CONDES DE BARCELONA
(128 C6) (*J 8*)

Splendid town palace from the *modernisme* period. Sun terrace, pool. The hotel offers a high level of comfort and genteel elegance on Barcelona's fanciest boulevard. *183 rooms | Passeig de Gràcia, 73–75 | tel. 9 34 45 00 00 | www. condesdebarcelona.com | Metro: Passeig de Gràcia (L2, L3, L4)*

DUQUESA DE CARDONA
(123 D5) (*J 11*)

Small Old Town hotel radiating discreet charm in a stylishly renovated 19th-century aristocratic palace. The 44 rooms vary greatly in size, and some of them have a view across the old harbour. Roof terrace. The hotel enjoys a very central location, only a few steps away from the Rambla. *Passeig Colom, 12 | tel. 9 32 68 90 90 | www.hduquesadecardona. com | Metro: Drassanes (L3)*

Colonial atmosphere and comfort at the H 1898, where Philippine tobacco used to be sold

H 1898 (122 C3) (*H 9*)

Today still, a touch of colonial style and tropical nostalgia can be felt in this palace of the former Philippine tobacco company, a comfortable hotel on the Rambla that boasts a pool on the roof terrace and a spa. *169 rooms | La Rambla, 109 | entrance Pintor Fortuny | tel. 9 35 52 95 52 | www.nnhotels.es | Metro: Catalunya (L1, L3)*

MAJESTIC ★ (128 C6) (*J 8*)

Barcelona's classic top hotel combines mod cons with the atmosphere of the 19th century on the Boulevard Passeig de Gràcia. Pool on the roof terrace. The *Drolma* gourmet restaurant has been awarded a Michelin star. *303 rooms | Passeig de Gràcia, 70 | tel. 9 34 88 17 17 | www.hotelmajestic.es | Metro: Passeig de Gràcia (L2, L3, L4)*

NERI (132 C3) (*J 10*)

This tastefully renovated 18th-century palace lies in the maze of alleyways of the Gothic Quarter, only a few paces from the cathedral on the atmospheric Plaça Neri. The elegant furnishings combine top comfort and hyper-modern design with velvet curtains and satin. The rooms in the historic building vary in size and amount of available light. *22 rooms | San Sever, 5 | tel. 9 33 04 06 55 | www.hotel neri.com | Metro: Jaume I (L4)*

OMM ★ (128 C5) (*J 7*)

The avant-garde wavy façade hides an oasis of minimalist design, exotic woods, high tech and feng shui. The spacious rooms with clear lines and natural materials are styled to within an inch of their lives and offer views of Gaudí's magnificent La Pedrera building. The **INSIDER TIP** big loft-like lobby is one of the most sought-after bars in Barcelona, the gourmet restaurant *Moo* a culinary and aesthetic experience. Roof terrace with pool, spa. *58 rooms | Rosseló, 265 | tel. 9 34 45 40 00 | www.hotelomm.es | Metro: Diagonal (L3, L5)*

PULITZER (122 C2) (*M H 9*)
You can't get more central than this, really: only a few paces away from Plaça de Catalunya. The minimalist design style is dominated by shades of white and grey. Pretty roof terrace lounge. Good level of service. *91 rooms | Bergara, 6–8 | tel. 9 34 81 67 67 | www.hotelpulitzer.es | Metro: Catalunya (L1, L3)*

SIXTYTWO HOTEL (128 C6) (*M J 8*)
Exclusive and elegant: the furnishings are super modern – in shades of brown and grey, with exotic woods and silk cushions – the service individually tailored to the guest. The courtyard boasts a Japanese garden. Make sure you ask for a room with an unimpeded view (from some all you'll see is a wall!). *45 rooms | Passeig de Gràcia, 62 | tel. 9 32 72 41 80 | www.prestigepaseode*

gracia.com | Metro: Passeig de Gràcia (L2, L3, L4)*

W HOTEL (O) (*M O*)
A trendy lifestyle and luxury hotel belonging to the W chain, situated on Barcelona's city beach. The mirror-like skyscraper in the shape of a gigantic sail was designed by star architect Ricardo Bofill. ⚡ Rooms and suites boast huge panorama windows with sea views. Add to this the *Eclipse Bar* on the 26th floor, gym, a fabulous spa, beach terraces with pool and gourmet restaurant. *473 rooms | Plaça de la Rosa dels Vents, 1 | tel. 9 32 95 28 00 | www.w-barcelona.com | Metro: Barceloneta (L4)*

HOTELS: MODERATE

ACTUAL (128 C5) (*M J 7*)
Modern-style design hotel, a few steps from the fancy boulevard Passeig de Gràcia. Ask for a room with a view of Antoni Gaudí's most famous house, La Pedrera. *29 rooms | Rosseló, 238 | tel. 9 35 52 05 50 | www.hotelactual.com | Metro: Diagonal (L3, L5)*

MARCO POLO HIGHLIGHTS

HOTELS: MODERATE

BANYS ORIENTALS ⭐
(123 E5) (ℳ J 10)
Architecture and design magazines praise this enchanting hotel within stylishly restored historic walls, centrally located between the Gothic Quarter and La Ribera. The small rooms with particularly large beds are furnished in minimalist style. Very good value for its location and comfort. *43 rooms | Argenteria, 32 | tel. 9 32 68 84 60 | www.hotelbanysorientals. com | Metro: Jaume I (L4)*

CATALONIA BORN (135 D3) (ℳ K 9)
Mid-range hotel in historic 19th-century building, centrally located in the trendy El Born quarter on Parc de la Ciutadella. Modern, comfortable rooms. *90 rooms |*

LUXURY HOTELS

Arts Barcelona ⭐ ☼
(135 F5) (ℳ L 11)
A dream of elegance, high-tech, design, sun and Mediterranean. In this avantgarde hotel tower (45 storeys) on the beach of the Olympic Village, expect generously sized rooms or suites with panoramic views and opulent marble bathrooms. Plus terraces, gardens, bars, cafés, spa, a swimming pool with sea view and the Arola tapas restaurant run by chef Sergi Arola, bearer of two Michelin stars. *482 rooms | from 385 euros | Marina, 19–21 | tel. 9 32 21 10 00 | www.hotelartsbarcelona.com | Metro: Ciutadella – Vila Olímpica (L4)*

Casa Fuster (128 C5) (ℳ J 7)
Listed luxury in one of the most beautiful buildings by Art Nouveau architect Lluís Domènech i Montaner, combining sumptuous modernisme decoration with all modern comforts. There's ☼ a panorama terrace too, as well as a pool, sauna and the Galaxó gourmet restaurant, plus the enchanting Café Vienés with its huge velvet sofas. *96 rooms | from 250 euros | Passeig de Gràcia, 132 | tel. 9 32 55 30 00 | www.hotelcasafuster.com | Metro: Diagonal (L3, L5)*

Miramar Barcelona ☼
(133 F5) (ℳ G 11)
High above Barcelona with breathtaking views across the city and out to sea; at the same time, this luxury hotel on the Montjuïc mountain lies only some ten minutes from the city centre! The building from the 1920s has been carefully renovated and equipped with the highest level of comfort and cutting edge design. Lovely gardens, terraces and pools. Gourmet restaurant Forestier. *75 rooms | from 220 euros | Plaza Carlos Ibañez, 3 | tel. 9 32 81 16 00 | www.hotelmiramar-barcelona.com | Metro: Plaça Espanya (L1, L3), then bus no. 50*

Mandarin Oriental (134 C1) (ℳ J 8)
Sophisticated mix of mega-modern design, timeless elegance and the Far East. From the exclusive rooms and suites you look onto the Art Nouveau façades of the Passeig de Gràcia or the pretty gardens. Spa, roof-top pool with panoramic views. Gourmet restaurant Moments run by female chef Carmen Ruscalleda, with three Michelin stars to her name. *91 rooms | from 325 euros | Passeig de Gràcia, 38–40 | tel. 9 31 51 88 88 | www. mandarinoriental.com | Metro: Passeig de Gràcia (L2, L3, L4)*

Arts Barcelona – avant-garde hotel tower with 45 storeys

Rec Comtal, 16–18 | tel. 9 32 68 86 00 | www.hoteles-catalonia.com | Metro: Arc de Triomf (L1)

CHIC & BASIC ★ (123 F4) (*⊞ K 10*)

Simply feel-good factor! Intelligent, creative, comfortable and cool: this light-filled design hotel is housed in a medieval palace, right in the heart of the hip Ribera quarter. Innovative interior design ideas and surprising details make this hotel a recommendation for unconventional travellers. *31 rooms (XXL, XL, L, M) | Princesa, 50 | tel. 9 32 95 46 52 | www.chic andbasic.com | Metro: Jaume I (L4)*

CONSTANZA (135 D1) (*⊞ J 8*)

A modern hotel with tasteful design and decorative details – from the lobby down to the rooms. Central location in the Art Nouveau quarter Eixample, near Plaça Catalunya. ☖ Lovely bar on the INSIDER TIP roof terrace. *46 rooms | Bruc, 33 | tel. 9 32 70 19 10 | www.hotelconstan za.com | Metro: Girona (L4)*

CONTINENTAL BARCELONA
(122 C3) (*⊞ H 10*)

This hotel is right on the Rambla. The rooms are furnished in a classical style, comfortably equipped (with fridges and microwave) and sound-insulation. Included in the price is a round-the-clock buffet with fresh fruit, salad, snacks and drinks. *35 rooms | La Rambla, 138 | tel. 9 33 01 25 70 | www.hotelcontinental. com | Metro: Catalunya (L1, L3)*

GRANVÍA (123 D1) (*J 9*)

While the rooms of this Art Nouveau palace have recently been renovated, the INSIDER TIP salons and breakfast rooms will make the heart of any fin-de-siècle fan beat faster. Pretty terrace. Central location. *53 rooms | Gran Vía de les Corts Catalanes, 642 | tel. 9 33 18 19 00 | www. nnhotels.es | Metro: Passeig de Gràcia (L2, L3, L4)*

ORIENTE (122 C4) (*H 10*)

This historic hotel counted Arturo Toscanini, Maria Callas and George Orwell amongst its guests. Today, the Belle Époque charm of the former grand hotel only remains in its dining and banquet room. *131 rooms | Rambla, 45–47 | tel.*

Former grand hotel: the Oriente

9 33 02 25 58 | www.husa.es | Metro: Liceu (L3)

PARK HOTEL (123 E5) (*K 11*)

Neither spa nor luxury, rather a gem of 1950s architecture: the once radical modern design of Antonio Moragas has been renovated and updated. The rooms vary greatly in size – the upper storeys offering a view across city and port. *91 rooms | Av. Marqués de l'Argentera, 11 | tel. 9 33 19 60 00 | www.parkhotelbarcelona.com | Metro: Barceloneta (L4)*

PRAKTIK (134 B1) (*J 8*)

Chic new design hotel in an Art Nouveau building, either with a view of the Rambla de Catalunya boulevard or of a pretty garden terrace. Modernisme architecture and modern furnishings. Comfortable and good value given the excellent location. *43 rooms | Rambla de Catalunya, 27 | tel. 9 33 01 30 79 | www.hotelpraktikrambla.com | Metro: Passeig de Gràcia (L2, L3, L4)*

SANT AGUSTÍ ⭐ (122 B–C4) (*H 10*)

This pretty hotel in a renovated 17th-century monastery lies on a typical square of the Raval neighbourhood and radiates rustic, romantic Old Town flair. Definitely ask for a room under the roof! *75 rooms | Plaça Sant Agustí, 3 | tel. 9 33 18 16 58 | www.hotelsa.com | Metro: Liceu (L3)*

HOTELS: BUDGET

BARCELONA URBANY
(136 A1) (*M 8*)

Trendy hostel with hotel-like comfort. The en-suite rooms all have air-conditioning and lockers. Roof terrace with panoramic views. Swimming pool, gym and free WiFi. Women-only rooms too. Prices include 'all you can eat' breakfast. *396* beds | *Meridiana, 97 | tel. 9 32 45 84 14 | www.barcelonaurbany.com | Metro: Glòries (L1)*

EL JARDÍ (122 C4) (*ⓜ J 10*)

Popular, completely renovated Old Town hotel on an enchanting square in the Gothic Quarter. The rooms are simple but all equipped with new bathrooms – the deal here is that the exterior rooms with a view are prettier but noisier. *40 rooms | Plaça Sant Josep Oriol, 1 | tel. 9 33 01 59 00 | www.eljardi-barcelona. com | Metro: Liceu (L3)*

HOSTAL GAT XINO (122 B3) (*ⓜ H 10*)

Stylish und funky: the rooms are all white and apple-green. All rooms with plasma screen, showers, heating and air-conditioning. Sun deck with chill-out area. Young, international ambience in the Raval neighbourhood. Prices incl. breakfast. *35 rooms | Hospital, 149–155 | tel. 9 33 24 88 33 | www.gatrooms.com | Metro: Sant Antoni (L2)*

HOSTAL GOYA (134 C2) (*ⓜ J 9*)

Familiar hostal only a few steps away from Plaça de Catalunya. The rooms have modern and cosy furnishings, with mosaic floors or wooden parquet, nearly all are en-suite. Free WiFi. *19 rooms | Pau Claris, 74 | tel. 9 33 02 25 65 | www.hostal goya.com | Metro: Plaça Catalunya (L1 L3)*

HOSTAL GRAU (122 C2) (*ⓜ H 9*)

Rustic hostal with wooden beam ceiling and fireplace in a typical Raval alley, near the Rambla. The rooms were restored in the past few years and the bathrooms modernised; the style has been kept classical and genteel. *20 rooms | Ramelleres, 27 | tel. 9 33 01 81 35 | www.hostalgrau. com | Metro: Catalunya (L1, L3)*

INOUT ALBERG (0) (*ⓜ 0*)

Amidst the natural park of Collserolla, eight times as big as New York's Central Park, by the way – and still only 15 minutes by suburban train into the city centre. Bar, swimming pool, playground and sports grounds. Separate modules of two to four beds with writing desk and fridge. All rooms have a WC, some a bath. 14–22 euros per person incl. breakfast. *158 beds | Major del Rectoret, 2 | tel.*

LOW BUDGET

▶ 19–25 euros is the price for double rooms (some en-suite) in the Garden House, a stately fin-de-siècle villa in the green residential quarter of Horta, only five minutes from the nearest Metro station. Garden, roof terrace, cosy lobby, guest kitchen. Familiar, easy-going atmosphere. Rooms are light and spacious. Bed linen, towels and WiFi are free, and there are women-only rooms too. *56 beds | (0) (ⓜ 0) Hedilla, 58 | tel. 9 34 27 24 79 | www.feetuphostels. com | Metro: Valldaura (L3)*

▶ *Hostal Girona* is a friendly family-run guesthouse in a stately Art Nouveau building: original mosaic floors, stucco ceilings and furnishings with the charm of times past. The rooms vary in size (doubles 45–62 euros), are renovated, have modern bathrooms, heating, air-conditioning and plasma screens; some have balconies. Rooms with windows giving on to the patio are quieter. *27 rooms | (135 D) (ⓜ K 9) Girona, 24 | tel. 9 32 65 02 59 | Metro: Urquinaona (L1, L4)*

9 32 80 09 85 | www.inoutalberg.com | suburban trains S1 and S2 Baixador de Vallvidrera, Vallvidrera

LA TERRASSA (122 B4) (*H 10*)
Low-budget place in the heart of Raval, not far from the Rambla. Half of the

hostaloliva.com | Metro: Passeig de Grà-cia (L2, L3, L4)

PASEO DE GRÀCIA (128 C5) (*J 7*)
The simply furnished rooms, partly with balcony or terrace, lie high above the fancy boulevard of Passeig de Grà-

Paseo de Gràcia: the hotel is right next to Gaudí's famous Casa Milà

rooms are en-suite, some have a balcony. Pretty courtyard. *42 rooms | Junta del Commerç, 11 | tel. 9 33 02 51 74 | www.la-terrassa-barcelona.com | Metro: Liceu (L3)*

OLIVA (134 C1) (*J 8*)
Friendly family guesthouse on the fourth storey of an Art Nouveau building on Barcelona's Passeig de Gràcia boulevard. All rooms have been tastefully renovated and the baths modernised. Very good value for this location. *16 rooms | Passeig de Gràcia, 32 | tel. 9 34 88 01 62 | www.*

cia (little noise), right next to Gaudí's famous Casa Milà. Ask for one of the *INSIDER TIP* rooms on the top floor. *33 rooms | Passeig de Gràcia, 102 | tel. 9 32 15 58 24 | www.hotelpaseodegracia. es | Metro: Diagonal (L3, L5)*

SAN REMO (123 E2) (*K 9*)
Well-kept family guesthouse in a pretty Art Nouveau house in Eixample, a few steps from the city centre. Very quiet, not only because of the double-glazed windows: the owner herself watches over

every guest's peace and quiet. *7 rooms |
Ausiàs Marc, 19 / Bruc, 20, 1st floor | tel.
9 33 02 19 89 | www.hostalsanremo.com |
Metro: Urquinaona (L1, L4)*

SOMNIO HOSTEL (134 B14) (*📖 J 8*)

Comfortable guesthouse on one floor
of an Art Nouveau building, only a few
metres from the fancy Passeig de Gràcia
boulevard. The style of the furnishings
is discreetly modern, with nice touches.
Good value given the exclusive location.
*27 beds | Diputación, 251, 2nd floor | tel.
9 32 72 53 08 | www.somniohostels.com |
Metro: Passeig de Gràcia (L2, L3, L4)*

THE PRAKTIK (135 D1) (*📖 K 8*)

Chic, comfortable and good-value: two-
star hotel in the Art Nouveau quarter
with modernisme mosaic floors and
modern interiors. All rooms en-suite,
heating and air-conditioning, some
with a balcony. Large sun terrace. Good-
value. *43 rooms | Diputación, 325 | tel.
9 34 67 31 15 | www.praktikhotels.com |
Metro: Girona (L4) or Tetuán (L2)*

APARTMENTS, BED & BREAKFAST

AMIGA BARCELONA BED & BREAKFAST (0) (*📖 J 3*)

This flat in a quiet location in the upper
part of town, in an Art Nouveau house
designed by Josep Puig i Cadafalch, is
tastefully furnished. Opulent breakfast.
Free WiFi. A double room costs 85 eu-
ros. *6 rooms | Gomis, 49 | 1st floor | tel.
6 36 83 25 84 (mobile) | www.barcelona-
bb.com | Metro: Vallcarca (L3)*

APARTAMENTOS SAGRADA FAMILIA (129 E4) (*📖 L 6*)

Light and modern apartments with two
bedrooms, salon, bathroom as well as
a fully equipped kitchen, located near

Gaudí's famous church in a residential
area with shops and restaurants. From
75 euros. *Ventalló, 4 | tel. 9 32 84 40 29 |
www.apartamentossata.com | Metro: Jo-
anic oder Alfonso X (L4)*

APARTMENTS RAMBLAS

Over 120 centrally located apartments for
every budget. The agency fee is included
in the price. *tel. 9 33 01 76 78 | www.
apartmentsramblas.com*

BARCELONA ROOM

Specialised in arranging private rooms
and apartments, all of which are regu-
larly checked. Personalised service.
Agency fee included in the price. *www.
barcelonaroom.com*

INSIDER TIP POBLENOU BARCELONA BED & BREAKFAST (136 B4) (*📖 N 11*)

All rooms in this lovely little guesthouse
are named after Spanish artists, such as
Dalí or Picasso – and vary accordingly in
design and creative details. All rooms
have a nice bathroom and plasma TVs. A
kettle with tea, coffees, and mineral water comes for free too. Fireplace lounge
and sun terrace. Pets allowed. 60–110
euros incl. breakfast. *10 rooms | Taulat,
30 | tel. 9 32 21 26 01 | www.hostalpob-
lenou.com | bus 41: Park del Poble Nou*

YOUTH HOSTEL

YOUTH HOSTEL BARCELONA SEA POINT 🔆 (134 C6) (*📖 J 12*)

This youth hostel is located on Barceloneta beach, about ten minutes on foot
from the city centre. The rooms have four
to eight beds and modern bathrooms.
Bike hire available. Overnight stay incl.
breakfast and internet access from 19
euros. *105 beds | Plaça del Mar, 4 | tel.
9 32 31 20 45 | www.seapointhostel.com |
Metro: Barceloneta (L4)*

Photo: Olympic stadium on Montjuïc

WALKING TOURS

The tours are marked in green in the street atlas,
the pull-out map and on the back cover

1 **A STROLL THROUGH
THE RIBERA QUARTER**

**Two hours between Santa
Maria del Mar, medieval
alleys, modern art and authentic Old
Town life. Watch out for pickpockets in
the back alleys of the Old Town! And try
not to choose a Monday for your wan-
derings, as many places are closed
then.**

Where in medieval times Barcelona's
craftsmen and tradesmen settled in
modest houses, today historic façades
shelter craft shops and galleries, eateries and bars – especially in the lower part
of the Ribera quarter, now trendy and
known as the El Born neighbourhood,
which reaches to Carrer Princesa. In the

adjoining Santa Caterina neighbourhood
up to the Sant Pere Més Baix alley, a new
cultural and bar scene is being established. In the upper part of the Ribera
quarter, Sant Pere, which ends on the
Sant Pere més alt alley with the famous
concert hall Palau de Música Catalana,
redevelopment and big changes are only
just starting.

Start your stroll on **Plaça de l'Àngel**
(*Metro: Jaume I, L4*), the city's former
wheat exchange. Take Carrer Argente-
ria, then the first side street to the left,
Carrer Vigatans, and you're right in the
picturesque maze of alleys that make up
the Ribera neighbourhood – and in the
historic centre of the textile and crafts
workshops.

The city supports young designers who

Old Town alleys and Mediterranean gardens:
a stroll through the picturesque Ribera, plus
splendid views from Barcelona's local mountain

set up shop in the medieval walls – which explains the many pretty shops here: in the tiny Carrer Esquirol, turning off left, and especially in the street of Banys Vells, which you reach through Carrer Grunyi. Follow the alley to the end, then turn left into Sombrerers.

Walking past the beautiful traditional general store of Casa Gispert → p. 73, you reach one of the neighbourhood's most impressive sights: the street of Montcada → p. 34 with its unique ensemble of Gothic palaces, museums such as the famous Picasso Museum → p. 34, and galleries. This is quite evidently where the other half of medieval society lived.

If you feel like a break, make yourself comfortable on the lovely patio of the Textil Café → p. 62, or have a glass of cava or wine in the more rustic and usually very crowded champagne bar El Xampanyet → p. 61. At the upper end of Carrer de Montcada you turn right into the Gran Cremat lane in order to reach Carrer Flassaders, where you can browse in charming shops behind historic façades.

Just before you hit Passeig del Born, to your right you'll see an odd (closed) passage: **Carrer Mosques**, the narrowest street in town. Look out for the small sculpture on the corner façade. This won't be the last time you've encountered such a curious bust: they used to point the way to the brothels of the quarter, close to the port.

In medieval times, **Passeig del Born** was the stage for tournaments and festivities; on weekdays the hemp shoemakers would set up their workbenches here. A few very pretty façades have been preserved and restored. Some of the cocktail bars here date back to the beginnings of the bar movement of the 1970s – and are still amongst the most popular in town. Rising behind Placeta Montcada, the church of **Santa Maria del Mar → p. 36** is Barcelona's most beautiful Gothic church. Definitely take the time to spend a few moments inside!

If you want to crown enjoyment of the arts with pleasures for the palate, you will find the wine bar *La Vinya del Senyor (closed Mon)* opposite, on the atmospheric plaça. Those interested in history should take a look at the remodelled square next to the church, with the **Fossar de les Moreres** monument commemorating the victims, buried here, of the Catalan-Castilian War, which ended in 1714 with the defeat of the Catalans. Take the picturesque Carrer Anisadeta to reach the street Canvis Vells. If you stand in front of the tiny Carrer Panses and take a closer look, you'll find another man's head on the façade above the entrance

Passeig del Born is lined with well-restored houses and trendy cocktail bars

arch of a residential house, which again used to point the way to prostitutes. Turn into the Carrer dels Ases – on your right-hand side you see the nicely restored **Plaça de les Olles**, which has kept the charm of centuries past. The aroma of fresh fish wafts across from the direction of **Cal Pep → p. 65**.

If you can resist this temptation, stay left, through Carrer Vidriera and the short Es-partería street, to reach Carrer Rec. This block has seen the opening of a number of hip fashion stores. At the end of the Vidriera alleyway you are looking at the magnificent, palace-like railway station [INSIDER TIP] *Estació de França,* the start-ing point in 1848 for the first steam lo-comotive in Spain. Take a look into the waiting hall clad in marble, steel and glass!

Go back along the street called Rec until you hit Passeig del Born again. This time, keep right, towards **Mercat del Born**: this is one of the prettiest market halls in town (dating back to the 19th centu-ry); an arts centre is scheduled to move in here soon. The hall is surrounded by pretty cafés and trendy bars; at the week-end late at night you have to fight your way through the party crowd.

Follow the street Commerç, past Plaça de l'Academia with the charming **Bar del Convent → p. 60**. Via Carrer dels Tiradors you reach one of the most at-tractive squares in the Old Town, **Plaça Sant Augustí Vell → p. 49**. Turning left, via Allada Vermell with its pretty bars, ca-fés and small-scale performance venues, walk through the typical Old Town alley of Assaonadors to Placeta d'en Marcús. The small chapel on the square is one of the few remaining examples of Roman-esque architectural heritage in Barcelona. Turn right into **Carrer dels Carders** with its small shops, cool bars and corner shops, then take one of the narrow alleys

to your left to Sant Pere més baix. The next stop is one of the most atmospheric squares in the neighbourhood: **Plaça de Sant Pere** with the Romanesque church of **Sant Pere de Puelles → p. 49**. **La Can-dela → p. 69**, the only café with outdoor seating here, is a good place to enjoy the idyllic scenery with a coffee or beer.

Walk along **Sant Pere més alt**, once a centre of the Catalan cloth trade – pro-duction took place a few steps on, in the first large cloth factories in Barcelona. At the end of the alley you find the mag-nificent Art Nouveau architecture of the **Palau de la Música Catalana → p. 31**. Carry on through a narrow side street, Verdaguer i Calis, with the lovely court-yard café **Bar de l'Antic Teatre → p. 60** and through the Freixures alleyway to the **Mercat de Santa Caterina → p. 49**, the spectacularly renovated market hall of the Ribera neighbourhood. Around the hall, modern bars and restaurants rub shoulders with long-established pubs and rustic eateries. Hungry? The **Cuines de Santa Caterina → p. 66** in the market hall come recommended.

Carrer Carders (Street of the Sailmakers) with a small, medieval-looking square where once the wool market was held, **Plaça de la Llana**, and Carrer Bòria take you back to Plaça de l'Ángel.

2 HEAD UP BARCELONA'S LOCAL MOUNTAIN: MONTJUÏC

This trip lasting several hours to Barcelona's local mountain leads you past some of the most impor-tant museums, treats you to breathtaking views of the city and provides a stroll through fairy-tale Mediterranean gar-dens. Be aware that on Sunday afternoons and Mondays the museums are closed! You can spend a couple of hours, but easily a whole day, too, on Barcelona's local mountain. The World Exhibition site of 1929 begins right behind Plaça de Espanya. Two campanile towers mark the *Sept–late April Fri and Sat 7–9pm, music and light show every half hour).*

In Avinguda de Marquès de Comilla, look

Architectural icon: the reconstructed World Exhibition pavilion of 1929

beginning of Avinguda de la Reina María Cristina. Flanked by water features and the exhibition pavilions, today used for trade fairs, it leads directly to the main façade of the National Palace (Palau Nacional) with the must-see **Museum of Catalan Art (Museu Nacional d'Art de Catalunya)** → p. 52, past the 'magic fountain' ● **Font Màgica**. Occasionally, on summer evenings, the huge Art Deco fountain provides a fascinating spectacle of water, light, colour and music *(May–Sept Thu–Sun 9–11.30pm, music and light show 9.30–11pm every half hour, mid-*

to your left to spot the INSIDER TIP *Pavil-ló Mies van der Rohe (daily 10am–8pm | admission 4.70 euros)*, which was designed by Bauhaus architect Mies van der Rohe in 1929 as the German pavilion for the World Exhibition and has been reconstructed to the original design. Hard to believe that this radically modern structure, which became an icon of 20th-century architecture, was built at the same time as the retrograde national palace! Diagonally opposite, you'll walk past the spectacular arts centre **Caixa Forum** → p. 50, a fabulously restored textile factory designed by Art Nouveau architect Josep Puig i Cadafalch. Carrying on uphill, the street leads past the open-air museum Poble Espanyol to Plaça de Sant Jordi. Here you can turn into Avinguda Montanyans, where stairways decorated with ceramics lead into Pg. de les Cascades and directly to the ☀ viewpoint in front of the **Museum of Catalan Art** → p. 52, from which you have a splendid panoramic view across Barcelona.

To your right, Pg. Santa Madrona winds its way uphill through the Mediterranean Jardins de Laribal, past the **Ethnological Museum (Museu Etnològic)** *(late Sept–late May Wed, Fri, Sun 10am–2pm, Tue, Thu, Sat 10am–7pm, June–late Sept Tue–Sat 10am–6pm, Sun 10am–2pm and 3–8pm | admission 3.50 euros | www.museuetnologic.bcn.cat)* onto Avinguda de l'Estadi. Another option is to take the escalators right behind the National Museum, leading through the Jardins de Joan Maragall gardens.

A quick detour to your right into Avinguda de l'Estadi leads to the **Estadi Olímpic (Olympic stadium)**, built in 1929 and completely renovated for the Olympic Games of 1992. You can't miss **Palau Sant Jordi**, an idiosyncratic sports palace reminiscent of a tortoise carapace, designed by star architect Arata Isozaki, and Santiago Calatrava's **Torre Calatrava (communications tower)**, rising like a bizarre needle into the sky.

Following Avinguda de l'Estadi in the opposite direction takes you to the **Fundació Joan Miró** → p. 51. Before your visit, you might like to stroll through the picturesque gardens of the 1929 royal pavilion of **Palacete Albéniz** *(only Sat, Sun and public holidays 10am–2pm | free admission)*. For the best views, head for the ☀ **Castell de Montjuic (fortress)** – either follow the signs on foot, or take the funicular. The station lies a few steps

from the Miró Foundation. Most attractions and paths are extremely well signposted, and maps of the area allow you to plan your walk as the fancy takes you. Behind the Olympic stadium, for example, you could visit the **Botanical Gardens (Jardí Botànic)** *(April, May and Sept daily 10am–7pm, June–Aug daily 10am–8pm, Oct–March daily 10am–6pm, Nov–Jan daily 10am–5pm | admission 3.50 euros, Sun from 3pm free and on the last Sunday of the month free | Dr. Font i Quer, 2 | www.jardibotanic.bcn.es)*. If you don't mind walking some more, head for the **Cementeri del Sud Oest**: in this cemetery lie not only Barcelona's leading citizens in splendid pantheons and Art Nouveau mausoleums, but also many normal people or victims of the Franco dictatorship who were executed in the fortress – in sad rows of grave niches. On the southern edge you'll find the grave of the famous anarchist Buenaventura Durruti.

A pleasant descent starting behind the Miró Foundation goes via the Escalera Generalife, an idyllic stairway with watercourses and fountains. At the end you're in the heart of the **Jardins del Teatre Grec**, the gardens around the reconstructed Teatre Grec amphitheatre. A recommendation for refreshments, a few steps away, is the romantic terrace of the **Font del Gat** café restaurant *(Tue–Sun 1–4pm, cafeteria to 6pm, in summer to 8pm | tel. 9 32 89 04 04)*.

End your walk via Passeig Santa Madrona and the street Lleida. A huge theatre complex, the Ciutat del Teatre, has grown up around the former flower market of **Mercat de les Flors**, and another World Exhibition pavilion opposite houses the **Archaeological Museum (Museu d'Arqueologia de Catalunya)** *(Tue–Sat 9.30am–7pm, Sun 10am–2.30pm | admission 3 euros | www.mac.es)*.

TRAVEL WITH KIDS

AQUÀRIUM (134 C5) (*J 11*)
The main attraction here is the large underwater tunnel allowing close-up views of sharks, octopus or sunfish. In the aquarium's interactive area, children may touch, listen to and discover the Mediterranean underwater world. *July and Aug daily 9.30am–11pm, Sept–June Mon–Fri 9.30am–9pm, Sat and Sun 9.30am–9.30pm | admission 17.50 euros, children 12.50 euros | Moll d'Espanya del Port Vell | www.aquariumbcn.com | Metro: Barceloneta (L4)*

BOSC DE LES FADES (122 C5) (*H 11*)
A fairy-tale forest, populated by gnomes, fairies and other fabled creatures, in an enchanted café, next door to Barcelona's Wax Museum. *Mon–Fri 10–1pm, Sat and Sun 10am–2pm | Passatge de la Banca, 5 | www.museocerabcn.com | Metro: Drassanes (L3)*

COSMOCAIXA (125 F3) (*H 3*)
In an interactive special department of the Science Museum, the youngest (3–9 years) discover phenomena such as weather, light and lasers, playing all the while. In the *Toca Toca!* area, children can feel their way around plants and animals in their habitats. *Tue–Sun 10am–8pm | admission 3 euros, children under 16 free | Teodor Roviralte, 55 | www.fundacio.lacaixa.es | FGC to Avinguda Tibidabo, then Tramvía Blau or on foot*

INSIDER**TIP** **EL REI DE LA MÀGIA** (123 E4) (*J 10*)
From witchcraft to Harry Potter: this shop has been selling everything magicians require for over a hundred years. Part of the setup is a small museum around magic arts. Guided tours include a performance with magic tricks *(Sat 6pm, Sun 12 noon)*. *Shop: Carrer Princesa, 11 | Mon–Fri 11am–2pm and 5–8pm, Sat 11am–2pm, museum:* (134 C4) (*F 91*) *Jonqueres, 15 | Sat 6–8pm and Sun 12 noon–2pm | admission 5 euros, with performance 12 euros | www.elreydelamagia.com | Metro: Jaume I (L4)*

JARDÍ JOAN BROSSA (133 E4) (*F 11*)
Enchanting park complex on Montjuïc with adventure playground, lawns for relaxing on, as well as space for playing football. Children learn to compose melodies in a playful way, jumping around on sound cushions or pedals. *Daily 10am – dusk | free admission | Metro: Espanya (L1, L3), then on foot or bus no. 55*

A huge aquarium and rollercoaster rides, chocolate and a fairy-tale forest: and that's not half of what Barcelona has to offer

MUSEU DE LA XOCOLATA
(135 D3) *(ｵ K 10)*

Chocolate tastings and all the history and myths surrounding cocoa. *Wed–Sat and Mon 10am–7pm, Sun 10am–3pm | admission 4.30 euros | Comerç, 36 | www.pastisseria.com | Metro: Jaume I (L4)*

MUSEU OLÍMPIC (OLYMPIC MUSEUM)
(133 D4) *(ｵ E 10)*

Pit yourself against athletics legend Carl Lewis: thanks to simulators and modern high-tech, knowledge is never dull in the interactive sports museum on Montjuïc. *Oct–March Tue–Sat 10am–6pm, April–Sept 10am–8pm, all year round Sun 10am–2.30pm | admission 4.05 euros, children under 14 free | Avinguda de l'Estadi, 60 (next to Olympic stadium) | www.museuolimpicbcn.cat | Metro: Espanya (L1, L3), then on foot or bus no. 55)*

PARC ZOOLÓGIC (135 E4) *(ｵ K 11)*

The zoo with large enclosures, dolphin shows and pony-riding lies in the Parc de la Ciutadella, where you can hire bike rickshaws or take a boat on to the lake. *Nov–Feb daily 10am–5pm, March–May and Oct daily 10am–6pm, June–Sept daily 10am–7pm | admission 16 euros, children (3–12 years) 9.60 euros | Parc de la Ciutadella | www.zoobarcelona.com | Metro: Marina or Arc de Triomf (L1)*

FUN PARK/MUSEUM OF DOLLS AND AUTOMATONS TIBIDABO
(125 F1) *(ｵ H 1)*

The fun park with panoramic views across Barcelona offers carousels, a Ferris wheel, rollercoaster and high-tech attractions. In the INSIDER TIP Museu dels Autòmates museums of dolls and automatons, one of the world's finest, children big and small can set mechanical toys in motion by pressing a button. *March–Dec, varying opening times | combined ticket admission 7–25 euros | www.tibidabo.es | FGC: Tibidabo, then Tramvía Blau and funicular*

FESTIVALS & EVENTS

Barcelona likes to party long and hard. While nearly all popular feasts have religious origins, what counts is the secular pleasure; the whole thing is usually rounded off by fabulous fireworks – not for nothing do the Catalans have a reputation for enjoying a bit of excess. Festivals and spectacular events fuel the desire to let it all hang out.

HOLIDAYS

1 Jan *(New Year)*; **6 Jan** *(Epiphany);* Good Friday; Easter Monday; **1 May** *(Labour Day);* Whit Monday; **24 June** *(Saint John' Days);* **15 Aug** *(Assumption of the Virgin);* **11 Sept** *(Catalan national holiday);* **24 Sept** *(La Mercè, patron saint of the city);* **12 Oct** *(Discovery of the Americas); 1 Nov (All Saints);* **6 Dec** *(Constitution Day);* **8 Dec** *(Immaculate Conception);* **25 Dec and 26 Dec** *(Christmas)*

FEASTS & FESTIVALS

JANUARY
▶ *Cavalcada de Reis:* splendid procession of the Three Wise Men through the city centre on 5 Jan.

MARCH
▶ *International vintage car rally:* magnificent automotive gathering between Barcelona and Sitges. *Tel. 9 38 94 93 57 | www.rallyesitges.com*
▶ *Marató Barcelona:* popular marathon run on the first Sunday. Start and finish: Plaça de Espanya. Booking up to 24 hours before the start. *Tel. 9 02 43 17 63 | www.barcelonamarato.es*

APRIL
▶ ★ *Sant Jordi (Day of the Book):* in honour of Saint George, patron saint of Catalonia, people give each other a red rose on 23 April. Books are sold on streets and squares, ten per cent cheaper than usual. The entire city seems to be out and about, in the centre and on the Rambla in particular.

MAY
▶ *Saló Internacional del Còmic:* major international comic fair. Mid-May. *www.ficomic.com*

JUNE
▶ INSIDER TIP *Sonar:* the *International Festival of Advanced Music and Multimedia Arts* is one of the leading avant-garde

Fantastic fireworks and gigantic human towers: the Catalans like to party fast and frequently

festivals: with contemporary sound art, techno music, net art and interactive installations. Mid-June. *www.sonar.es*

▶ ★ **Nit de Sant Joan:** the whole city celebrates the shortest night of the year (23/24 June) with jumps over bonfires and a big fireworks display

▶ **Primavera Sound:** this music event is among the largest Indie rock festivals in Europe, a mega event. *www.primavera sound.com*

JULY/AUGUST

▶ **Grec:** this international arts festival puts on concerts, theatre and dance, featuring stars as well as performances by interesting newcomers. *Tel. 9 33 01 77 75 | www.barcelonafestival.com*

▶ **Festa Major de Gràcia:** for a popular neighbourhood party in Gràcia, the streets and squares get spectacular decorations. The events include concerts and dance performances, theatre and processions, as well as street artists and activities for children. The neighbours put tables and chairs out in front of their houses, rivers of wine and beer flow. *www.festamajordegracia.cat*

SEPTEMBER

▶ ★ **Festa de la Mercè:** popular feast honouring Barcelona's patron saint in the days around 24 Sept. Experience ● *castells* (human towers), the procession of the *gegants* (giant figures), fire-spewing dragons, dancing devils and spectacular fireworks. *www.bcn.es/merce*

OCTOBER TO DECEMBER

▶ **International Jazz Festival:** concerts in the Palau de la Música Catalana, the Auditorium and Luz de Gas. *www.theproject.es*

DECEMBER

▶ **Fira de Santa Llùcia:** the Nativity and Christmas market takes place around Advent time in front of the Gothic cathedral from early Dec to 23 Dec

LINKS, BLOGS, APPS & MORE

LINKS

▶ www.lecool.com/barcelona Barcelona's off-the-wall culture for insider – all cool and usually not too expensive either

▶ barcelona.guialowcost.es/ Whether sights, live music, festivals or tai chi: a reliable source of information on what you can do for little money or even for free in Barcelona (in Spanish)

▶ www.barcelonaparties.com Virtual party guide and the right guest lists to get you into the most exclusive clubs in town

▶ http://www.easycatalan.com/ Who said English-speakers never make an effort to learn the local language? Spend a few hours on this online Catalan language primer and amaze the locals!

▶ http://www.barcelona-life.com Very handy city guide, not only for expats

▶ www.barcelona-metropolitan.com Information about the most important events of the month, insightful articles, tips and reviews – and much more

BLOGS & FORUMS

▶ barcelonareviewed.blogspot.com/ 'Barcelona – The Good, The Bad and The Ugly' is the title of this wide-ranging blog on Catalan culture – with critical observations on architecture, bars, restaurants

▶ www.barcelonaphotoblog.com Lots of photos, interesting links, fun comments from the fields of culture, culinary, and the curious.

▶ http://www.youtube.com/watch?v=6r4_2uMpzKI Short youtube best-of video of FC Barcelona's epic 6:2 victory over Real Madrid. The Catalan goal commentary gives a nice aural insight into the language too!

▶ www.spottedbylocals.com/barcelona/ Barcelona off the beaten tourist track, in the footsteps of the locals: up-to-date insider tips and shared experiences

Regardless of whether you are still preparing your trip or already in Barcelona: these addresses will provide you with more information, videos and networks to make your holiday even more enjoyable.

VIDEOS

▶ www.videosfrombarcelona.com/videos A local lady takes you to well-known and less well-known neighbourhoods, to important sights, hidden favourite places, shopping and typical celebrations and festivals. Refreshing, fun and knowledgeable, Gina tells stories from her life and day-to-day life in her city and gives practical advice too. Thanks to Gina, you'll know your way round before even touching down

▶ www.calarumba.com Information on the Catalan rumba scene in Spanish. Under the keyword 'Videos' you'll find up-to-date as well as historic recordings with the leading representatives of Barcelona's modern city folklore

APPS

▶ Independently of an online connection, the free iTune GuidePal cityguide app guides you reliably through the city jungle, following the tried and trusted categories Eat & Drink, Nightlife, Shopping, etc

▶ Whether museums, parks, restaurants, tapas bars, events, hotels or travelling with children – the Top 10 Barcelona smartphone app has many helpful tips, recommendations, information and pictures, as well as an easy-to-navigate menu, street and Metro maps, plus interesting links

▶ Use www.tmb.cat, the website of the municipal transport provider, to download a free app (look for the keyword Mobile & PDA), which will lead you to the nearest bus, Metro, suburban train station or tram stop

NETWORKS

▶ www.couchsurfing.org/ This 3-million-strong online hospitality network has a strong representation in Barcelona. Even if you already have accommodation, it's a cool tool for meeting the locals

▶ http://www.dopplr.com/place/es/barcelona Travellers exchange their experiences about where's best to eat, drink or sleep in Barcelona

TRAVEL TIPS

ARRIVAL

✈ Flight prices vary significantly; with a bit of luck you'll find return tickets from London from £50. Flight time from London is about two hours. Ryanair (*www.ryanair.com*) will get you cheaply to Girona (Gerona in Catalan), an approx 90-min shuttlebus ride from the city (single 12, return 21 euros). The major North American airlines offer direct flights to Barcelona. While price-wise it might be cheaper to go via London to catch one of the many budget flights from the London hubs, consider whether it is worth the additional time and hassle factor. The Aerobus lines A1 (Terminal 1) and A2 (Terminal 2) take you into town. They leave every 10 min *(Mon–Fri 6am–1am, Sat, Sun from 6.30am)* to Plaça de Catalunya via Sants railway station and Plaça de Espanya and back *(Mon–Fri 5.30am–0.15am, Sat, Sun from 6am | 5.05 euros, return ticket 8.75 euros | approx. 30–45 minutes)*. Between 11pm and 5am, the N17 night bus (Nitbus) commutes every 1.5 hours between Plaça de Calatunya and the airport. A direct rail connection from the airport to Estació de França (via Sants railway station and Passeig de Gràcia, approx. every half hour, duration 20–30 min, 3 euros, departures 6.08am–11.38pm). A taxi costs at least 27 euros; the airport surcharge is 3.10 euros.

🚆 Direct trains come in from Paris, Milan and Zurich.

🚗 The main route by car crosses the French-Spanish border at Ceret/La Junquera.

BANKS & CREDIT CARDS

Most banks are open during the week between 8am and 2pm, some on a Saturday too up to 1pm (not July/August!). Savings banks *(caixas)* also open Thursdays between 4.30 and 7.45pm. The numerous ATMs/cash points accept debit and major credit cards. Emergency number for blocking credit cards: Visa: *tel. 900 99 11 24,* Mastercard: *tel. 900 97 12 31.*

CONSULATES & EMBASSIES

UK EMBASSY
Torre Espacio | Paseo de la Castellana 259D | 28046 Madrid | http://ukin spain.fco.gov.uk

US EMBASSY
Paseo Reina Elisenda de Montcada, 23 | 08034 Barcelona | tel. 932 80 22 27 | http://barcelona.usconsulate.gov

RESPONSIBLE TRAVEL

It doesn't take a lot to be environmentally friendly whilst travelling. Don't just think about your carbon footprint whilst flying to and from your holiday destination but also about how you can protect nature and culture abroad. As a tourist it is especially important to respect nature, look out for local products, cycle instead of driving, save water and much more. If you would like to find out more about eco-tourism please visit: *www.ecotourism.org*

From arrivals to weather

Holiday from start to finish: the most important addresses and information for your trip to Barcelona

CUSTOMS

Within the EU goods for personal use may be imported and exported (e.g. 800 cigarettes, 90 litres of wine, 10 litres of spirits) without paying duty. For US citizens entering the EU, the quantities are lower, e.g. a maximum of 200 cigarettes, 2 litres of alcoholic beverages below 15 per cent alcohol by volume and 1 litre above 15 per cent.

EMERGENCY

National emergency number: *tel. 112* | local numbers: police *tel. 0 88* or *tel. 0 92* | fire service *tel. 0 80* | emergency doctor *tel. 0 61*

EVENTS GUIDES & CITY MAGAZINES

Every Thursday sees the publication of *Guía del Ocio*, the Spanish-language events guide *(also online: www.guiadelociobcn.es)*. The English-language monthly magazine *Metropolitan* can be picked up from many cinemas and bars *(www.barcelona-metropolitan.com)*. The Spanish-English lifestyle magazine *b-guided* is available online at *www.b-guided.com*.

EXPLORING THE CITY

BARCELONA CARD

Discounts: Metro and bus gratis, discounts of up to 50 per cent for museums, events, sightseeing. Tickets for two/three days 27.50/33.50 euros, 4 days 38 euros, 5 days 45 euros. They are for sale at the airport terminals T1 and T2 and at the tourist information on Plaça de Catalunya, at the main railway station and the city hall or at *www.barcelonaturisme. com* (10 per cent online discount!).

BIKE RICKSHAWS

Guaranteed eco-friendly, the chauffeured Trixi rickshaws can take you to all sights. The drivers know the routes off the beaten track too. Short trips from 6 euros. Trixis can be requested on the street, or pick you up from your hotel; alternatively book one of the guided tours: from 15 euros for 30 minutes. 150 euros will get you the use of the rickshaw incl. driver for eight hours. Prices are always for two people! *Daily midday–8pm | in front of cathedral | www.trixi.com*

BIKE TOURS AND HIRE

Check the tourist office website for current offers of various companies: *www. barcelonaturisme.com | tel. 9 32 85 38 32* *Budget Bikes* offer guided tours, incl.

BUDGETING

Coffee	1.20 euros	for an espresso
Shoes	from 9.50 euros	for linen shoes
Wine	4 to 8 euros	for a bottle of house wine
Cinema	from 8 euros	for a ticket
Snack	2.50 euros	for a serving of patatas bravas
Taxi	from 90 cents	per kilometre

in English, from 22 euros, and hire out bikes from several branches *(from 9 euros for 2 hours, 19 euros per day incl. insurance)*. *Daily 10am–8pm | Unió, 22* (134 B4) *(⟁ H 10) | Metro: Liceu (L3); Estruc, 38* (134 C2) *(⟁ J 9) | Metro: Catalunya (L1, L3); Passeig de Borbó, 80* (132 C6) *(⟁ J 12) | Metro: Barceloneta (L4) | tel. 9 33 04 18 85 | www.budget bikes.eu*

BUS TURÍSTIC

Double-decker buses with a hop-on-hop-off system cover all the important sights every 15 to 30 minutes. Departures from the tourist office on Plaça de Catalunya from 9am *(day pass 23 euros, two-day pass 30 euros)*. A tour through night-time Barcelona *(June–Oct 9.30pm–midnight)* costs 17.50 euros.

GOCAR TOURS ☺

Discover the city by GoCar and GPS – in an environmentally-friendly way: all CO_2 emissions are neutralised in cooperation with reforestation projects managed by the *Carbon Neutral Company*, a leading European environmental protection agency. *GoCar* (123 E4) *(⟁ J 10) Freixures, 23 | opposite Santa Caterina market | tel. 9 02 30 13 33 | www.gocartours.es | Metro: Jaume I (L1)*

GUIDED WALKS

The tourist office organises various walks: through the Gothic Quarter *(daily 10am in English and Sat midday in Spanish | 13 euros)*, in the footsteps of Pablo Picasso *(Tue, Thu, Sat 4pm in English and Sat 4pm in Spanish | 19.50 euros incl. entrance to Picasso Museum)*, monuments of *modernisme (Oct–May Fri and Sat 3pm, June–Sept Fri and Sat 6pm in English and Sat in Spanish | 13 euros)* and a gourmet tour *(Fri and Sat 10am in English and Sat 10.30am in Spanish | 19.50 eu-*

ros). Varying thematic tours and literary walks. *Meeting point: tourist office Plaça de Catalunya* (123 D2) *(⟁ J 9) | www.barcelonaturisme.com | Metro: Catalunya (L1, L3)*

HARBOUR TRIP ●

Two great ways to explore Barcelona's old port or the Universal Forum of Cultures: the comfortable *golondrinas* barges, and aboard one of the new glass-bottomed catamarans that depart behind the Columbus monument (122 B6) *(⟁ H 11)*. *Tel. 9 34 42 31 06 | www.lasgolondrinas. com | Metro: Drassanes (L3)*

INLINE SKATE TOURS

On a Friday, hundreds of night owls roll through Barcelona. Anyone who can steer and brake is allowed on – for free. Barcelona's skater association organises various routes, led by 'stoppers' in reflective clothing. Gear can be hired. *Start: 10.30pm |* (135 E5) *(⟁ L 11) Centre de la Vila | Salvador Espriu, 61 | www.patinarbcn.org | Metro: Ciutadella – Vila Olímpica (L4)*

One of the largest Spanish skate shop chains offers guided tours through the city or along the beaches *(1 hr 10 euros, 2 hrs 15 euros, 3 hrs 20 euros)*. *Inercia Skate Shops |* (135 E3) *(⟁ K 10) Roger de Flor, 10 | tel. 9 34 86 92 56 | www.inercia-shop.com | Metro: Arc de Triomf (L1)*

SCOOTER TOURS

Guided scooter tours, also in English, are available from 40 euros. Good-value scooter hire from 36 euros for 1 day, 3 days 85 euros (incl. insurance). Inliners 5 euros per hour, 15 euros per day, electric skateboards 10 euros per hour, hire from the *Cooltra* shop near the beach promenade. (134 C6) *(⟁ J 11) Pg. de Joan Borbó, 80–84 | tel. 9 32 21 40 70 | www.cooltra.com | Metro: Barceloneta (L4)*

If you prefer going solo you can get a good idea of the thematically organised route suggestions on the tourist office's website. Under the heading 'Barcelona Metro Walks' seven more routes are described in detail – by Metro and on foot – off the beaten tourist track, with maps and two-day ticket for all public transports (12.50 euros). *Tourist office below Plaça de Catalunya or at terminals T1 and T2 at the airport | www.barcelona turisme.com*

HEALTH

Thanks to the European social security agreement, EU citizens enjoy free health insurance; bring your European Health Insurance Certificate (EHIC). You'll have more choice however with a travel health insurance policy, which is vital for North American citizens. As a private patient you will receive faster and more comprehensive service and can get the money back later. Medical emergency services for first-response care *(Centros de Asistencia Primaria)* are found in all parts of town. For details phone the information line *tel. 010.*

IMMIGRATION

British and US citizens need their passport; EU citizens only need their ID card.

INFORMATION BEFORE YOU GO

TOURIST OFFICE OF SPAIN
– *22–23 Manchester Square | London W1U 3PX | tel. 020 74 86 80 77 | www.spain.info*
– *666 Fifth Avenue | 35th Floor | New York, NY 10103 | tel. 212 26 58 822*
– *8383 Wilshire Blvd | Suite 960 | Beverly Hills CA 90211 | tel. 0323 65 87 188*

INFORMATION & ACCOMMODATION ONLINE
– *www.barcelona-online.com:* tourist information, accommodation, last-minute offers, comprehensive service
– *www.barcelona-on-line.es:* guesthouses, hotels and apartments, last minute too
– *www.oh-barcelona.com:* agency with over 800 hotel rooms and apartments on their books
– *www.hotelsbcn.com:* hotel rooms

INFORMATION IN BARCELONA

CITY OF BARCELONA
General information on all kinds of practical questions: *tel. 010 | www.bcn.es*

CURRENCY CONVERTER

£	€	€	£
1	1.10	1	0.90
3	3.30	3	2.70
5	5.50	5	4.50
13	14.30	13	11.70
40	44	40	36
75	82.50	75	67.50
120	132	120	108
250	275	250	225
500	550	500	450

$	€	€	$
1	0.70	1	1.40
3	2.10	3	4.20
5	3.50	5	7
13	9.10	13	18.20
40	28	40	56
75	52.50	75	105
120	84	120	168
250	175	250	350
500	350	500	700

For current exchange rates see www.xe.com

TURISME DE BARCELONA/ MUNICIPAL TOURIST OFFICE

Excellent, comprehensive information, incl. many city walks, on the *www. barcelonaturisme.com* website. *Daily 9am–9pm* | (123 D2) (∭ J 9) *below Plaça de Catalunya, entrance opposite Corte Inglés department store* | *tel. 9 32 85 38 34 (daily 8am–8pm, incl. in English)* | *Metro: Catalunya (L1, L3)*

TOURIST OFFICE CATALAN GOVERNMENT

Mon–Sat 10am–7pm, Sun 10am– 2.30pm | (128 C5) (∭ J 7) *Passeig de Gràcia, 107* | *Palau Robert* | *tel. 9 32 38 80 91* | *www.gencat.cat/palau robert* | *Metro: Diagonal (L3, L5)*

POLICE

By ringing *tel. 112* and at the main station of the *Policia Nacional* you benefit from a round-the-clock interpreting service. (123 D3) (∭ J 9) *Via Laietana, 43* | *tel. 9 32 90 30 00* | *Metro: Urquinaona (L1, L4)*. All stations provide multilingual forms for reporting a crime.

POST

Stamps can also be bought at a tobacco shop *(estanc)*. The postage for cards and letters within Europe is 65 cents, 78 cents to North America.

WEATHER IN BARCELONA

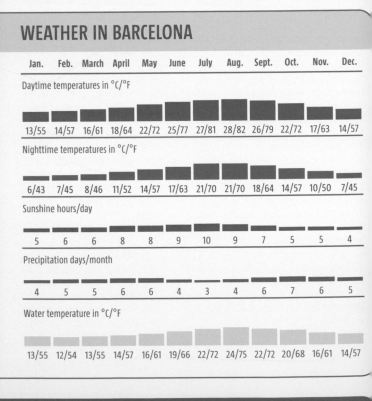

	Jan.	Feb.	March	April	May	June	July	Aug.	Sept.	Oct.	Nov.	Dec.
Daytime temperatures in °C/°F	13/55	14/57	16/61	18/64	22/72	25/77	27/81	28/82	26/79	22/72	17/63	14/57
Nighttime temperatures in °C/°F	6/43	7/45	8/46	11/52	14/57	17/63	21/70	21/70	18/64	14/57	10/50	7/45
Sunshine hours/day	5	6	6	8	8	9	10	9	7	5	5	4
Precipitation days/month	4	5	5	6	6	4	3	4	6	7	6	5
Water temperature in °C/°F	13/55	12/54	13/55	14/57	16/61	19/66	22/72	24/75	22/72	20/68	16/61	14/57

Most phone boxes only work with telephone cards now, available from tobacco shops *(estancs)* and from post offices *(correus)*. Prepaid cards for mobiles are relatively expensive in Spain, so check whether you're better off with your home provider's roaming charges. A cheaper option are the call-by-call cards for sale in Chinese and Pakistani shops or telephone shops. Text messages are a cheaper alternative to phoning. High costs are incurred by checking voicemail: you're best off turning it off while still at home!

Dialling code for UK: 0044, for North America 001, then the local dialling code without the zero. Dialling code for Spain: 0034. There are no dialling codes within Spain.

PUBLIC TRANSPORT

A cheap and fast way to get around is by Metro, which runs between 5am and midnight from Mon to Thu, as well as on Sun and public holidays, Fri to 2am, Sat around the clock. A single journey costs 1.45 euros, a carnet of ten tickets (T10) 8.25 euros, where you have the choice between various Metro lines, bus, night bus (Nit Bus) and the suburban train FGC *(day pass 6.20 euros, two-day pass 11.50 euros, three-day pass 16.50 euros)*.

From Metro station Parallel (L3), the *Funicular de Montjuïc* will take you up to Avinguda de Miramar; from there by cable car to the citadel of Montjuïc *(Telefèric de Montjuïc | April, May, Oct 10am–7pm, June–Sept 10am–9pm, Nov–March 10am–6pm | 6.50 euros)*. The jetty at the old port and Montjuïc are connected by cable car *(Transbordador del Port | mid-Oct–Feb daily 11–5.30pm, March–May and June–mid-Sept daily 11am–8pm, mid-Sept–mid-Oct daily 11am–7pm | 9 euros)*.

To get up the Tibidabo, take the *Tramvía Blau* museum tram from FGC station Av. Tibidabo *(mid-June–mid-Sept and Easter holidays daily 10am–8pm, Easter–mid-June and mid-Sept–Oct Sat and Sun 10am–8pm, Nov–Easter Sat and Sun 10am–6pm | 2.90 euros, return trip 4.50 euros | www.emt-amb.com)*, from which you change into the *Funicular del Tibidabo (Mon–Fri 10.45am–5pm, Sat, Sun 10.45am–8pm | 4 euros)*.

When there's no tram, the Av. Tibidabo Metro station and the Tibidabo are connected by bus no. 196 *(daily to 10pm, Mon–Fri every quarter of an hour, at weekends every half hour)*. Information: *tel. 010* or in the *Metrostation Universitat | tel. 9 33 18 70 74 | www.tmb.net*

THEATRE & CONCERT TICKETS

Reservation and credit-card bookings: *Entrada Caixa Catalunya | tel. 9 02 10 12 12* or *Servi Caixa | tel. 9 02 33 22 11 | www.serviticket.com*

TIPPING

In restaurants, hotels, etc., a tip of five to ten per cent is the norm. In bars and restaurants, the tip is placed on the little plate with the bill/check.

WIFI

Most hotels and guesthouses, also public institutions such as libraries, museums or markets and many parks (watch out for the blue 'W' sign) are equipped with free WiFi. More and more bars and cafés too are now offering WiFi (look out for 'Free WiFi').

USEFUL PHRASES CATALAN

PRONUNCIATION

c	like "s" before "e" and "i" (e.g. Barcelona); like "k" before "a", "o" and "u" (e.g. Casa)
ç	pronounced like "s" (e.g. França)
g	like "s" in "pleasure" before "e" and "i"; like "g" in "get" before "a", "o" and "u"
l·l	pronounced like "l"
que/qui	the "u" is always silent, so "qu" sounds like "k" (e.g. perquè)
v	at the start of a word and after consonants like "b" (e.g. València)
x	like "sh" (e.g. Xina)

IN BRIEF

Yes/No/Maybe	Sí/No/Potser
Please/Thank you/Sorry	Sisplau/Gràcies/ Perdoni
May I ...?	Puc ...?
Pardon?	Com diu *(Sie)*?/Com dius *(Du)*?
I would like to .../	Voldria .../
Have you got ...?	Té ...?
How much is ...?	Quant val ...?
I (don't) like this	(no) m'agrada
good	bo/bé *(Adverb)*
bad	dolent/malament *(Adverb)*
Help!/Attention!/Caution!	Ajuda!/Compte!/Cura!
ambulance	ambulància
police/fire brigade	policia/bombers
Prohibition/forbidden	prohibició/prohibit
danger/dangerous	perill/perillós
May I take a photo here/of you?	Puc fer-li una foto aquí?

GREETINGS, FAREWELL

Good morning!/afternoon!	Bon dia!
Good evening!/night!	Bona tarda!/Bona nit!
Hello!/Goodbye!	Hola!/Adéu! Passi-ho bé!
See you	Adéu!
My name is ...	Em dic ...
What's your name?	Com es diu?

Parles Català?

"Do you speak Catalan?" This guide will help you to say the basic words and phrases in Catalan.

DATE & TIME

Monday/Tuesday	dilluns/dimarts
Wednesday/Thursday	dimecres/dijous
Friday/Saturday	divendres/dissabte
Sunday/working day	diumenge/dia laborable
holiday	dia festiu
today/tomorrow/	avui/demà/
yesterday	ahir
hour/minute	hora/minut
day/night/week	dia/nit/setmana

TRAVEL

open/closed	obert/tancat
entrance/driveway	entrada
exit/exit	sortida
departure/	sortida/
departure/arrival	sortida d'avió/arribada
toilets/restrooms /	Lavabos/
ladies/gentlemen	Dones/Homes
Where is ...?/	On està ...?/
Where are ...?	On estan ...?
left/right	a l'esquerra/a la dreta
close/far	a prop/lluny
bus	bus
taxi/cab	taxi
bus stop/	parada/
cab stand	parada de taxis
parking lot/	aparcament/
parking garage	garatge
street map/map	pla de la ciutat/mapa
train station/harbour	estació/port
airport	aeroport
schedule/ticket	horario/bitllet
train / platform/track	tren/via
platform	andana
I would like to rent ...	Voldria llogar ...
a car/a bicycle	un cotxe/una bicicleta
petrol/gas station	gasolinera
petrol/gas / diesel	gasolina/gasoil
breakdown/repair shop	avaria/taller

FOOD & DRINK

Could you please book a table for tonight for four?	Voldriem reservar una taula per a quatre persones per avui al vespre
on the terrace	a la terrassa
The menu, please	la carta, sisplau
Could I please have ...?	Podria portar-me ...?
bottle/carafe/glass	ampolla/garrafa/got
salt/pepper/sugar	sal/pebrot/sucre
vinegar/oil	vinagre/oli
vegetarian/	vegetarià/vegetariana/
allergy	allèrgia
May I have the bill, please?	El compte, sisplau

SHOPPING

Where can I find...?	On hi ha ...?
I'd like .../	voldria/
I'm looking for ...	estic buscant ...
pharmacy/chemist	farmacia/drogueria
baker/market	forn/mercat
shopping center	centre comercial/gran magatzem
supermarket	supermercat
kiosk	quiosc
expensive/cheap/price	car/barat/preu
organically grown	de cultiu ecológic

ACCOMMODATION

I have booked a room	He reservat una habitació
Do you have any ... left?	Encara té ...
single room	una habitació individual
double room	una habitació doble
breakfast/half board	esmorzar/mitja pensió
full board	pensió completa
at the front/seafront	exterior/amb vistes al mar
shower/sit down bath	dutxa/bany
balcony/terrace	balcó/terrassa

BANKS, MONEY & CREDIT CARDS

bank/ATM	banc/caixer automàtic
pin code	codi secret
cash/	al comptat/
credit card	amb targeta de crèdit
change	canvi

HEALTH

doctor/dentist/paediatrician	metge/dentista/pediatre
hospital/emergency clinic	hospital/urgència
fever/pain	febre/dolor
inflamed/injured	inflamat/ferit
plaster/bandage	tireta/embenat
ointment/cream	pomada/crema
pain reliever/tablet	analgèsic/pastilla

POST, TELECOMMUNICATIONS & MEDIA

stamp/letter/postcard	segell/carta/ postal
I need a landline phone card	Necessito una targeta telefònica per la xarxa fixa
I'm looking for a prepaid card for my mobile	Estic buscant una targeta de prepagament pel mòbil
Where can I find internet access?	On em puc connectar a Internet?
Do I need a special area code?	He de marcar algun prefix determinat?
socket/adapter/charger	endoll/adaptador/carregador
computer/battery/ rechargeable battery	ordinador/bateria/ acumulador
at sign (@)	arrova
internet address	adreça d'internet (URL)
e-mail address	adreça de correu electrònic
e-mail/file/print	correu electrònic/fitxer/imprimir

LEISURE, SPORTS & BEACH

beach	platja
sunshade/lounger	para-sol/gandula

NUMBERS

0 zero	12 dotze	60 seixanta
1 un/una	13 tretze	70 setanta
2 dos/dues	14 catorze	80 vuitanta
3 tres	15 quinze	90 noranta
4 quatre	16 setze	100 cent
5 cinc	17 disset	200 dos-cents/dues-centes
6 sis	18 divuit	1000 mil
7 set	19 dinou	2000 dos mil
8 vuit	20 vint	10000 deu mil
9 nou	30 trenta	
10 deu	40 quaranta	½ mig
11 onze	50 cinquanta	¼ un quart

NOTES

STREET ATLAS

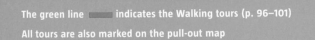

The green line ▬▬ indicates the Walking tours (p. 96–101)
All tours are also marked on the pull-out map

Photo: Olympic Park

Exploring Barcelona

The map on the back cover shows how the area has been sub-divided

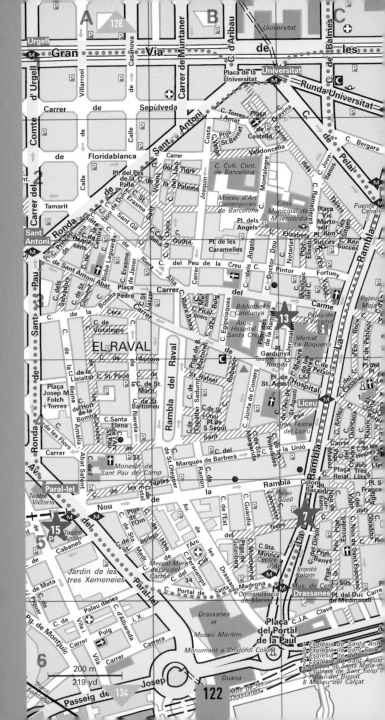

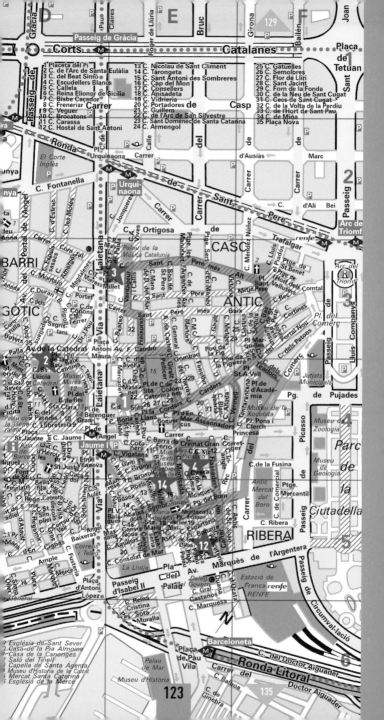

Passeig de Gràcia

Corts Catalanes

Carrer Casp

El Corte Inglés

C. Fontanella

Urquinaona

Ronda

BARRI GOTIC

Palau de la Música Catalunya

CASC

ANTIC

Arc del Triomf

Arc de Triomf

Pl. del Comerç

Museu Picasso

RIBERA

Parc de la Ciutadella

Museu de Zoologia

Museu de Geologia

Antic Mercat del Born

Estació de Franca renfe RENFE

Passeig de la Circumval·lació

Barceloneta

Ronda Litoral

Palau de Mar

Museu d'Història

123

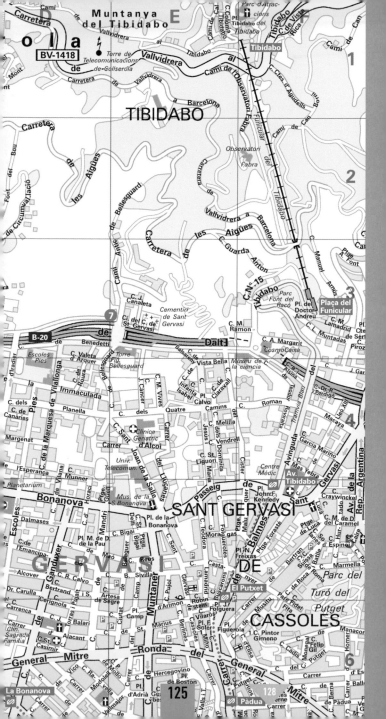

Pge. M.
Auxiliador
C. de
l'Aprestadora
Buenos
Badal
C. d'Olzina
Noguera
Ferreria
Palla
C. d'Alpens
LA
C. de Toledo
C. J.
Vinassa
Bravo
BORDETA
Quetzal
Carrer   de   Viladec   del   Corral
Gavà
Camí
de la Cadena
Caserna de
Lepant
Ptge.
de
Marçal
Amadeu Oller
Mossèn
B. Pi
Magòria
La Campana

Carretera
del Prat
C. Aprestadora
General
Admiradé

C. de
l'Amnistía
Pl. D'Ildefons
Gerdà
Física
Gran   Via   de   les
Química
Pl. de les
Matemàtiques
Parc
de la Font
Florida
C. Sta.
Dorotea

Carrer   de   la
Mercat Municipal
del Port
Parc de
Can
Sabaté
EL
POLVORÍ
Mare de Deu
de Port
Narbion
Llorca
S A N T S
Estadi
Joan
Serrahíma
Plaça
de Sant
Jordi
Av. del Marquès
Poble
Espanyol
Pl. Pare
E. Millán

Carrer
de
Fís
Franca
M O N T J U I C
Av. dels Montanyà

2 de
nòfol
de la
Mecànica
la
Zona
Franco
Foneria
C. del Túria
C. del Guadalete
Ptge. del Llobregat
C. de Fortuna
C. de Iecla
C. del Guadalquivir
C. de l'Anoia
C. de la Muga
Estadi
La Vinya
Estadi
Julià de
Campmany
3
La
Fuixarda
Institut Nacional
d'Educació
Física de Catalunya
(INEFC)
Piscines
Bernat
Picornell

1 C. de F. Boix i Campo
2 C. de Soweto
3 C. de Gernika
Jardins de
l'Arboreda
Forns
C. de Cata...
Av.
N. C. Av.
Franco
Ptge. Clos
Pl. Alta de
Can Clos
Plaça
d'Europa

C. del Llobregat
Carrer
del
Ferrocarrils
CAN
CLOS
Can
Clos
C. de la Maître
Camp de
Beisbol
M u n t a n y
Torre de
Telecomunicacions

Carrer
Camí
L'Esparver
C. Pedrera del Mussol
Carretera
Fontana
les Banderes
Anella
Palau
Sant
Jordi

Passeig
de
Carrer
de Sant Eloi
C. dels
C. Negrell
Foc
Carrer
P
Olímpica
d e

Piscina
del Cisell
C. de
l'Encuny
C.
Estadi
La Bàscula
Carrer
Estadi
d'Hoquei
Pau Negre

Parc del
Fossar
de la
Pedrera
Auditorio
sot del
Migdia
Mirador
del
Migdia
Antic de l'Anim
Jardi
M o

C. de
Gabriel Miró
C. de Torres
de Marina
Carrer
Mare
Camí
de Ferrocarrils Catalans
Cementiri del
Sud Oest

Motors
5

B-10
Deu
CAN TUNIS
Camí
del

C.
de
Port
Montjuïc
19
de
Can
Tunis

6
250 m
273 yd
N
Circumval·lació
C. Galtés
de
Passeig
132
Carretera   de   Circumval·lació

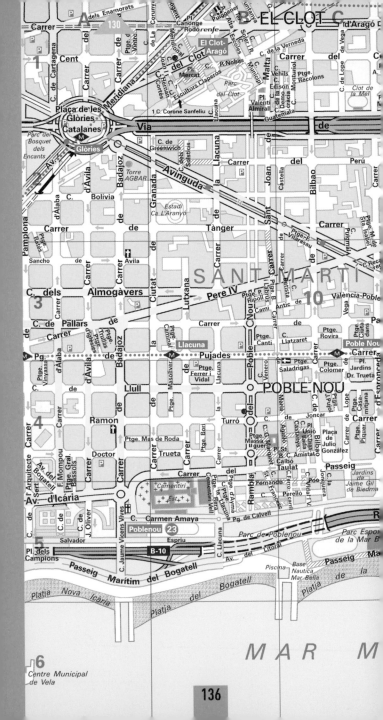

SANT MARTI

POBLE NOU

MAR M

The index includes a selection of the streets and squares shown in the street atlas.
The numbers in brackets represent street names on the city-centre map, p. 122/123
Av. = Avinguda | C. = Carrer | Pl. = Plaça | Pg. = Passeig

STREET INDEX

KEY TO STREET ATLAS

Autobahn Motorway (Freeway)		Autoroute Autostrada
Vierspurige Straße Road with four lanes		Route à quatre voies Strada a quattro corsie
Bundes- / Fernstraße Federal / trunk road		Route fédérale / nationale Strada statale / di grande comunicazione
Hauptstraße Main road		Route principale Strada principale
Fußgängerzone - Einbahnstraße Pedestrian zone - One way road		Zone piétonne - Rue à sens unique Zona pedonale - Via a senso unico
Eisenbahn mit Bahnhof Railway with station		Chemin de fer avec gare Ferrovia con stazione
U-Bahn Underground (railway)		Métro Metropolitana
Buslinie - Straßenbahn Bus-route - Tramway		Ligne d'autocar - Tram Linea d'autobus - Tram
Information - Jugendherberge Information - Youth hostel		Information - Auberge de jeunesse Informazioni - Ostello della gioventù
Kirche - Sehenswerte Kirche Church - Church of interest		Église - Église remarquable Chiesa - Chiesa di notevole interesse
Synagoge - Moschee Synagogue - Mosque		Synagogue - Mosquée Sinagoga - Moschea
Polizeistation - Postamt Police station - Post office		Poste de police - Bureau de poste Posto di polizia - Ufficio postale
Krankenhaus Hospital		Hôpital Ospedale
Denkmal - Funk- oder Fernsehturm Monument - Radio or TV tower		Monument - Tour d'antennes Monumento - Pilone radio o TV
Theater - Taxistand Theatre - Taxi rank		Théâtre - Station taxi Teatro - Posteggio di tassì
Feuerwache - Schule Fire station - School		Poste de pompiers - École Guardia del fuoco - Scuola
Freibad - Hallenbad Open air - / Indoor swimming pool		Piscine en plein air - Piscine couverte Piscina all'aperto - Piscina coperta
Öffentliche Toilette - Ausflugslokal Public toilet - Restaurant		Toilette publique - Restaurant Gabinetto pubblico - Ristorante
Parkhaus - Parkplatz Indoor car park - Car park		Parking couvert - Parking Autosilo - Area di parcheggio
Stadtspaziergänge Walking tours		Promenades en ville Passeggiate urbane
MARCO POLO Highlight		MARCO POLO Highlight

INDEX

All sights and destinations mentioned in this guide as well as some important streets and squares, names and concepts are listed in this index. Page numbers in bold refer to the main entry.

WRITE TO US

e-mail: info@marcopologuides.co.uk

Did you have a great holiday? Is there something on your mind? Whatever it is, let us know! Whether you want to praise, alert us to errors or give us a personal tip – MARCO POLO would be pleased to hear from you. We do everything we can to provide the very latest information for your trip.

Nevertheless, despite all of our authors' thorough research, errors can creep in. MARCO POLO does not accept any liability for this. Please contact us by e-mail or post.

MARCO POLO Travel Publishing Ltd
Pinewood, Chineham Business Park
Crockford Lane, Chineham
Basingstoke, Hampshire RG24 8AL
United Kingdom

PICTURE CREDITS
Cover Photograph: Sagrada Família (Laif: Knechtel)
Images: BarcelonaTurisme (17 bottom); W. Dieterich (68 l.); DuMont Bildarchiv: Pompe (flap l., 2 bottom, 3 top, 3 centre, 3 bottom, 7, 42, 46/47, 50/51, 58/59, 69, 70/71, 78/79, 80, 86/87, 104, 105, 109, 120/121); ECOsèries: Toni Jiménez (16 bottom); © fotolia.com: Galina Barskaya (16 centre); R. Freyer (2 centre top, 8, 9, 18/19, 25, 54, 60, 64, 109 bottom); R. M. Gill (33, 38, 56, 94, 98, 102, 103); R. M. Gill und Salvador Dali, Gala-Salvador Dali Foundation/VG Bild-Kunst, Bonn 2007 (57); Huber: Lubenow (12/13); © iStockphoto.com: jiri jura (16 top); Laif/hemis.fr: Borgese (52), Jacques (2 centre bottom, 26/27), Moirenc (41); Laif/Le Figaro Magazine: Martin (6, 82/83, 108 top); Laif: Gonzales (85), Knechtel (1 top, 63), Lange (74/75), Selbach (92), Siemers (2 top, 5), Stukhard (49), Tophoven (24 r.); Look: age fotostock (96/97), age fotostock/Succesion Picasso/VG Bild-Kunst Bonn 2011 (22/23), Fleisher (88), Pompe (15), Stumpe (102/103), The Travel Library (10/11); Look/Arcaid: Clapp (100); D. Massmann (1 bottom); mauritius images: AGE (72), Alamy (flap r., 77), Pixtal (68 r.); mauritius images/ imagebroker: Lescourret (4); D. Renckhoff (20, 24 l., 30, 34, 37, 66, 91); Vaho works S.L (17 top), T. P. Widmann (104/105); E. Wrba (45)

1st Edition 2012
Worldwide Distribution: Marco Polo Travel Publishing Ltd, Pinewood, Chineham Business Park, Crockford Lane, Basingstoke, Hampshire RG24 8AL, United Kingdom. Email: sales@marcopolouk.com
© MAIRDUMONT GmbH & Co. KG, Ostfildern
Chief editors: Michaela Lienemann (concept, managing editor), Marion Zorn (Concept, text editor)
Author: Dorothea Massmann · Editor: Karin Liebe
Programme supervision: Ann-Katrin Kutzner, Nikolai Michaelis, Silwen Randebrock
Picture editor: Gabriele Forst
What's hot: wunder media, Munich; Cartography street atlas: © MAIRDUMONT, Ostfildern; Cartography pull-out map: © MAIRDUMONT, Ostfildern
Design: milchhof : atelier, Berlin; Front cover, pull-out map cover, page 1: factor product munich
Translated from German by Kathleen Becker, Lisbon; editor of the English edition: John Sykes, Cologne
Phrase book in cooperation with Ernst Klett Sprachen GmbH, Stuttgart, Editorial by Pons Wörterbücher
All rights reserved. No part of this book may be reproduced, stored in a retrieval system or transmitted in any form or by any means (electronic, mechanical, photocopying, recording or otherwise) without prior written permission from the publisher.
Printed in Germany on non-chlorine bleached paper.

DOS & DON'TS ☝

These things are best avoided in Barcelona

DRIVING IN BARCELONA

You're best off leaving the car at home (or at least in the garage). While the road system has been expanded, during rush hour everything comes to a grinding halt. Parking spaces in the city centre are scarce, car parks expensive, not to mention parking offences. Never leave valuables in the car! And if somebody signals to you that there is something wrong with your car, don't on any account stop! Watch out at red lights, in the city centre in particular! One will distract you while his colleague quick as lightning, cleans out the back seat or grabs the bag from the passenger seat. Don't leave anything in sight! Close the back windows, lock the doors. Whatever you do, don't get out of the car! Recently, Barcelona has seen an alarming increase in this kind of attack. Should you lose your car keys, better change the lock – these gangs operate at international level.

SMOKING

Smoking is prohibited in all public spaces, restaurants, bars and clubs. With rare exceptions, smoking is only allowed outside the door or on terrace cafés.

UNDERESTIMATING PICKPOCKETS OR MUGGERS

Unfortunately, due to the serious increase in muggings and pick-pocketing, you should exercise extreme caution these days while walking through town. Rather than keeping money and credit cards in your handbag, carry them (invisibly) on your body (passport best as a photocopy!). In the Old Town in particular, petty criminals lie in wait even in the daytime. They usually work as a team: while one will distract you, the other rips the bag off your shoulder or neck. At night, avoid the dark and narrow lanes of the Old Town, and even the Metro. A travel guide immediately outs you as a tourist: drop the book discreetly into your bag.

SIGHTSEEING IN BEACHWEAR

Visiting a church in shorts or with a bare midriff is not considered good style in Catalonia and can nowadays even incur a fine! In restaurants, bars or hotel lounges too, visitors in flip-flops, shorts and little socks will earn a condescending smile at best. And pickpockets spot you as a tourist a mile away.

FALLING FOR FRAUDSTERS

Decline any invitation to a spot of gambling: you can only lose! Organised gangs operate in the Rambla area in particular. Don't allow yourself to be shepherded into 'cheap' shops – quality has its price, whether in Barcelona or elsewhere. Supposedly 'typical' souvenirs often turn out to be 'made in Taiwan' and the authentic flamenco show might be an expensive tourist trap.